Praise for

# *Life Is Funny Until It's Not*

"I love calling Chonda my friend. I am so proud of her for digging in and sharing her story with others. Her story is a testimony of how to love God through all of life's messes, heartache, and celebrations. Anyone who knows Chonda's story knows how amazing she is at making you laugh—but what you'll read in this book is the depth of her heart and ministry. It's awesome."

—**Michael W. Smith,** three-time Grammy Award winner with thirty-one #1 hit songs

"Chonda Pierce is a master storyteller recounting the harsh events of her life as the springboard to sheer hilarity in this brutally honest memoir. Chonda's book provides hope and encouragement to those who feel that the deep hurts in their lives are beyond redeemable. Proverbs 17:22 says that 'A cheerful heart is good medicine, but a crushed spirit dries up the bones.' This book is great medicine!"

—**Mike Huckabee,** former governor of Arkansas, Fox News host, and two-time presidential candidate

"This book is a must-read for fans of clean comedy and all comedy. Chonda's gripping story brings laughter to tears and tears to laughter. This book is an amazing read."

—**Tim Hawkins,** top-selling Christian comedian

"Raw, real, gut-wrenching, funny, bold, courageous, hopeful—Chonda style. This book will change conversations and lives. It's a gift to us all."

—**Dr. Tim Clinton,** president of the American Association of Christian Counselors

"*Life Is Funny Until It's Not* reveals Chonda's story from her heart and perspective. Many of her books have given a glimpse into different stages of her life. This book invites you into an intimate look into all of it. She gives us permission to see the dark places and the beautiful spaces of her very being. God created her to be a vibrant, fun, and loving person that shares His love. As a comedian, she has shown His light from stage for over thirty years. Readers now get to see His light as she shares all of her story in an attempt to help you with healing your own story. 'Therefore confess your sins to each other and pray for each other so that you may be healed. The prayer of a righteous person is powerful and effective' (James 5:16). I'm praying over all that read this honest account to experience healing."

—**Tracey Robison,** LPC-MHSP, clinical director of Branches.org

# LIFE IS FUNNY
## UNTIL IT'S NOT

# LIFE IS FUNNY
## UNTIL IT'S NOT

A Comic's Story of Love, Loss, and Lunacy

CHONDA PIERCE

Skyhorse Publishing

Skyhorse Publishing books may be purchased in bulk at special discounts for sales promotion, corporate gifts, fund-raising, or educational purposes. Special editions can also be created to specifications. For details, contact the Special Sales Department, Skyhorse Publishing, 307 West 36th Street, 11th Floor, New York, NY 10018 or info@skyhorsepublishing.com.



Visit our website at www.skyhorsepublishing.com.
Please follow our publisher Tony Lyons on Instagram @tonylyonsisuncertain

10 9 8 7 6 5 4 3 2 1

Library of Congress Cataloging-in-Publication Data is available on file.

Cover design by John Caruso
Cover photo by Diego Brawn

Print ISBN: 978-1-68451-523-3
eBook ISBN: 978-1-5107-8142-9

Printed in the United States of America

*For Sawyer and Connor*

# CONTENTS

# FOREWORD

One of my dear and most cherished friends is the "Queen of Clean Comedy," Chonda Pierce. She's the bestselling female comedian of all time with her recordings of comedy shows, and she packs sold-out venues across the country where devoted audiences spend a couple of hours laughing so hard as to trigger an epidemic of incontinence. (The cost of cleaning the upholstered seats in the theaters and auditoriums where she performs surely must be factored into the cost of the facility!)

Like many comedians, she is a master storyteller as she recounts harsh events of her life as the springboard to sheer hilarity. Most comedians are funny because they tell stories we can relate to—stories that are close enough to our own experiences that we feel better knowing the comedian is as weird as we are.

Chonda has that special "weirdness."

Chonda is insanely funny largely because she's just as weird as we know ourselves to be. Her stories are unique to her, but it's easy to feel she's been hacking our emails to get material that sure sounds like our own families. That's the secret of a great comic—telling stories that make us feel they could be our own stories (even when we are glad that they are NOT!).

*Life Is Funny Until It's Not* is Chonda's personal story. There's signature "Chonda-funny" stuff, but in this brutally honest memoir,

Chonda shares the deep pain and personal darkness that gave birth to the material we just think is funny.

Her raw candor can be uncomfortable at times, but her journey serves to provide hope and encouragement to those who feel that the deep hurts in their lives are beyond redeemable.

Her story reveals anything but a life of "winging it" and living on the carefree side of the street. Her story has more personal potholes than a Minnesota highway at the end of winter. Yet it's a story of looking for and shining light on the very darkest places of the human experience. Through a lifetime of challenges that would cause most of us to curl into a fetal position and give up, Chonda holds nothing back in describing a tough journey that consistently is about an authentic faith that won't let her quit and keeps her on her feet.

Some of the best and most effective medicine I've ever taken wasn't given to me by a doctor, but by a comedian. Laughing releases endorphins into our system that have tremendous healing properties. The Bible says that "A cheerful heart is good medicine, but a crushed spirit dries up the bones" (Proverbs 17:22). This book is great medicine!

If you are as big a Chonda fan as I am, you'll appreciate understanding how her comedy comes from the pits of personal challenges. But more importantly, she doesn't spill her soul to make you feel bad for her. This is not a pity-party book whining about the rough spots. This is a book to help you find the same quality and power of hope that you already find in her hilarious performances.

I loved her already, but after reading her story, I not only love her even more—I love God even more for bringing her through the low places to put her in the high places!

—Mike Huckabee
former governor of Arkansas

# AUTHOR'S NOTE

I have been working on this book for more than sixty years. Of course, I didn't know how to write or spell during a few of those years, much less type, and personal computers weren't even invented. Nevertheless, here we are.

I have often said on stage that when I die, I want my tombstone to read, "There was an elephant in the room, and she talked about it." Truth is, I've never really talked much about the elephants in my own life. You know, those big giant pains in the you-know-what or the flashing warning signs in your subconscious telling you that what you are about to do is probably not a good idea. Yes, this book is filled with those.

Most of you will be okay with my story. Some will be surprised, and many will be appalled. I am sad for those. No one wants to work in this public world of entertainment in Christian ministry for thirty years just waiting for the chance to tick someone off and disgust supportive followers. No, I wish I could tell you I was born again at age four. Called into ministry at sixteen. Married a true iconic Christian leader at twenty-three, and here we are. Nope. My life did not unfold that way. And at the same time, life has a way of moving on, no matter how you handle it. Life is funny... until it isn't.

My girlfriend Melanie asked me, "Why do you want to write all this now? Why not just let it all go and put it behind you?" She has a point. And believe me, there won't be another book about any of this again!

At this stage in my career and in my personal life, I decided it was simply important to me that you know the truth as I see it, and my truth is not always pretty.

I have spent over thirty years in the public eye of professional Christendom. Pedestals in Christianity trouble me. So, I decided that you need to know that the funny gal on stage, the one you have blessed with your support and laughter for more than thirty years, was not always perfect. I didn't want my story to be told as if I was some kind of saint, some godly woman who did everything right every time. I'm pretty sure you have already discovered that for yourself, but I needed to say it.

More importantly, I need someone else besides you to hear me say it. It's that other "elephant in the room," and this one, I just can't talk about. My daughter. She is beautiful and smart. My firstborn. But she has asked for privacy, and so because of her desire to remain out of my life, she will remain the "elephant in the room."

The Apostle Paul said in 2 Corinthians 12:5, "I will not boast about myself, except about my weaknesses." He goes on to say in verse 7, "Therefore, in order to keep me from becoming conceited, I was given a thorn in my flesh, a messenger of Satan, to torment me." I don't think my "thorn" is a messenger from Satan. But I guarantee you, it is a force of destruction of my spirit—my outlook—that Satan has used to be my undoing.

But listen up! The rest of that passage in 2 Corinthians is the thesis of this entire book. Are you ready? "Three times I pleaded with the Lord to take it away from me. But he said to me, 'My grace is sufficient for you, for my power is made perfect in weakness'" (vv. 8–9).

Paul continues to talk about boasting in his weakness. I'm not quite content with the boasting part yet. It has taken a myriad of counselors, pastors, and friends to make me even remotely comfortable with my failings. Paul can delight in hardships. I just find a way to joke about them. Paul delights in persecutions. I just delete them from Facebook! Paul says, "when I am weak, I am strong." I say, when I am weak, I am pretty stinking funny.

And somewhere in the mix, there is YOU.

Thank you for reading along. Thank you for more than thirty years of laughs and love. Not sure how much longer I will go at this. (We will see if I have an audience left after this book!)

And to my "elephant in the room," I love you and will love you until my dying breath.

## CHAPTER 1

# PREACHER'S DAUGHTER

As a middle child in a pastor's family, I was as rebellious and independent as they come. You know, the kind of kid who puts her hand on the stove, gets reprimanded, then goes back to put her hand on the stove again. I questioned authority and got in trouble often for doing things my own way. Like the time I rode my bike to the Piggly Wiggly and spent the money for my piano lesson on candy instead of going upstairs to my piano teacher's room above the store.

"Chonda, you're going to hell in a handbasket." My grandma's words still echo in my mind. Nanny was the meanest Christian I've ever known—strict and rigid to extremes. Okay, that's exaggerated. But it plays well on stage! The truth behind the joke? Nanny was a saint. Oh, she was strict and ultra conservative, but her eldest daughter (my aunt)? *She* was the meanest Christian I've ever known. (Okay, that's a bit of an exaggeration—but she had her moments, believe me!) I combined the two because when I told this story, one was alive and one was dead. And it's not gossip if they're dead. It's just *history*!

Nanny wore her hair up, her skirt down, and the Tower of Babel stacked on top of her head. She loved God and loved her family with an iron fist. She'd make us kids go outside to get our own switch. I know Nanny went to Heaven, but I'm certain she doesn't live on the same street as Jesus, because if her attitude had anything to do with it, there's no way she lives on His street.

My dad was a Church of the Nazarene pastor. In the early days of that denomination, the rules of conduct were extremely strict. I'm talking long skirts, no makeup, no music, and no dancing—which makes for one boring senior prom night! It also made me a chronic rule-breaker.

When I was ten, I bought a transistor radio shaped like a mouse head. I thought it was so cute. Later I discovered it was Mickey Mouse. I'd never even heard of Mickey Mouse because we didn't watch television. We had a small TV set in the living room, but we kept a blanket over it so no one in the church would know about it. (In case you're wondering why we had a TV but didn't watch it, it was for the same reason I have a treadmill but have never been on it.) Appearances trumped authenticity.

I used to hide that radio under my bed and wait until my parents went out so we kids could turn it on and dance the night away. One day, we pulled the radio out, cranked it up as loud as it would go, then wrapped wet paper towels up and down the bottom half of our legs to pretend we were wearing go-go boots. We danced the hours away until Three Dog Night blared the opening line of their song "Joy to the World." My sisters, Charlotta and Cheralyn, and I stopped and gasped. Jeremiah in *my* Bible was no bullfrog. We turned the radio off because we realized Dad had been right all along: rock and roll music will send you to Hell! In fake go-go boots, no less.

I was born in Covington, Kentucky, but I grew up in a whole series of small towns in South Carolina. My close friends might say I technically never grew up, but I'll leave it to you to determine which side of that debate you're on. My family lived in Rock Hill, Georgetown, Orangeburg, and Myrtle Beach, with a few years in Indiana and Kentucky interspersed here and there. We moved every three or four years, but the house in Myrtle Beach holds the best and worst memories for me. Let's just say my formative years were in the small towns of South Carolina as the daughter of a preacher man.

My dad was a confusing man, to say the least. On one hand, he was a great dad. He could fix anything and build anything. He taught me how to change the oil in a car and swing a hammer before I was twelve. And he taught me how to fish. I can put a grub worm onto the hook on a cane pole or on a spinner rod. (I know, but sometimes you gotta do what you gotta do to reel in a big one!) I can take the fish off the hook and filet it for supper or nail a catfish to the side of a tree and skin it for the deep fryer. Most of the time, I was his buddy. For some reason, of four kids, I was the one he chose to do all his tinkering with. Early on, I could identify an Allen wrench and needle nose pliers, and I could guess which socket he would need to loosen the bolt before he even told me. I learned a lot of good things from Dad. I miss *that* dad. I will always miss *that* dad.

Then, there was the other dad. It seemed like the fun dad, the kind and helpful dad, disappeared every few months. In his place, the dad none of us wanted to be around would appear. When I was little, the "switch" would often catch me by surprise. I'd hop off the bus, race to the garage or grab a fishing pole, and run to find Dad. "Daddy! I'm home. And I know exactly what you've been waiting on! Me! Let's go fishing!"

Like the flip of a switch, he would look at me as if I were a stranger. "Get to your room. Do homework. You are the last person I want to see today."

As preachers go, I think he was top of his class. He had charisma and was a master of hellfire and brimstone preaching. I think he often thought everything and everyone outside the church was a danger, and he had the scripture references to back it all up. But that *other* dad—the bad dad—had both a temper and a wandering eye. For someone who believed in the literal words of the Bible, he had a very poor sense of boundaries. Come to think of it, I inherited a lot from my dad. In fact, a 23andMe DNA test would show I'm 83 percent mixed European and 17 percent no boundaries. Suffice to say that's why we moved around a lot—always one step ahead of the church committee or an angry husband.

In his book *The Pastor's Kid: Finding Your Own Faith and Identity*, Barnabas Piper, son of Pastor John Piper, wrote that the church congregation wants the preacher's kid to dress like a grandparent and behave like Jesus—but they also seem to want the times when the pastor's daughter makes out and the son drinks beer. Remember Dusty Springfield's song "Son of a Preacher Man"? Trust me, that preacher's son was looking for the preacher's daughter.

I know a lot of preachers' kids. Many rebelled while they were growing up. A few turned around and became pastors and preachers themselves. Others? Well, there are some who have not darkened the door of a church since they left home. I call it the "Stained Glass Jungle." On the plus side, the pressures of a congregation of people peering into our parsonage, coupled with our own growing family dysfunctions, resulted in some amazing comedy material for me. On the minus side, it led to some painful therapy. Looking back, I think the therapists should be writing more books about the perils of children of professional Christians. But then again, it would probably put a lot of "professional" Christians out of ministry.

We Courtney kids (my maiden name) used to dress alike. McCall's 2243 was our pattern—long drawstring skirts, because elastic was too worldly. Wearing that skirt was hard on my brother, Mike. And yes, he hates that joke. I'm not sure if he hates that I insinuate he wore a skirt, or if he can't stand that I have made a better living for myself by telling people he wore a skirt.

I find it fascinating that two people can be raised by the same parents and turn out so completely different—at least on the surface. Then again, look at Jesus and His brother James. Jesus became the Lord and Savior; James ran a yogurt shop in Bethlehem.

Okay, stop for a minute. Don't get upset. That's a joke about James. I'm not being blasphemous. It's only a joke. Of course, if Jesus had a Jewish brother, he wouldn't have run a yogurt shop; he would have been His agent. (Relax, that's another joke!)

The difficult times in our childhood manifested in my life very differently than they did in my brother's. My brother never really talked much to me about our childhood. Maybe we *all* learned how to keep secrets—secrets he never shared from our childhood and secrets we created of our own. Me? I have oozed mine out onstage and in therapy for over thirty years.

One memory my brother and I do share with others (and remember the same way) is family prayer time. At the end of the day, Mom and Dad would gather us around the couch, and we kids would then have to say our evening prayers. Mike, the oldest and the only boy, would give a mini sermon with perfect voice inflection complete with scripture references. All he lacked was a closing verse of "Just as I Am" and he could have "saved" me again. Charlotta would pray tenderly for missionaries and starving children, and Cheralyn would pray the classic, "Now I Lay Me Down to Sleep."

Me? I spent my time with Jesus confessing anything and everything I could think of. "Lord, I found a cigarette butt in the woods today. I wanted to light it, but I'm not allowed to have matches. Forgive me for trying anyway."

Yep! I was rebelling and confessing all at an early age. Ditching the rules was in my DNA. Did I ever get caught? Constantly. If there had been a *Cops* television reality show for pastors' kids back then, you would have seen the church police driving up to my house with sirens blaring during every episode.

A knock on the door, and then... "Chonda, come out with your hands up and get those paper towels off your legs."

Then, with the neighbors watching, they'd march me straight into that handbasket to hell my grandma was always talking about. Nanny once told me and four of my cousins we were all headed to hell in that handbasket together. Which made me wonder just how big that handbasket is.

But it was in that rule-breaking that the seed of who I am today got planted, because I found out that if I could make my mom laugh when she caught me, I'd get in a lot less trouble. And that eventually led me to the stage.

Now my dad, whew! Hope your chair is comfortable. (Or if you're reading this on the commode, that it's a padded seat.) Laughter didn't really work on him. Well, some days it did. I think that's the hard part. God only knows the mystery of how I survived the dance around Dad. Some days I got a laugh, most days I got nothing. Often his response to my mere existence was the belt, which he used often. You've heard the phrase, "This is going to hurt me more than it does you," right? I never believed that, and neither should you. Think about it. A tall adult man, sliding the belt off his pants, wielding it like a whip, and then bringing it crashing down on the thin, frail buttocks of a pre-teenage girl. Come on, that hurt me a *lot* more than it hurt him. (Yes, back then I actually had frail buttocks.)

Most often, if one of us kids was getting a whooping, we all got one. Dad would line us up, fling off his belt, and start whipping. I am not sure what was more painful for me, the belt making contact and leaving red stripes and welts on my body or listening to it make contact on my brother's and sisters' backsides. In retrospect, I wish I'd had the extra natural padding I have today back then. Dad might have broken his belt.

Some days when we knew it was coming, we would put on all our underwear to soften the sting of the leather, and sometimes with enough pairs of drawers on, we could even take some of the sting out of the metal buckle. Then afterwards we would go to the bathroom and drop our drawers to compare who got hit hardest. That was one contest in which I never minded coming in fourth place. Occasionally, Dad would tell us to drop our drawers completely to the floor *before* our whippings. On those days, we all lost.

Did I mention there were four of us kids? Mike was almost ten years older than me, Charlotta was four years older, I was next, and Cheralyn was three years younger than me. That leads to the inevitable question. How did I end up with the name Chonda? Family legend has it that my parents took the words Chevy and Honda and blended them. If that's true, I'm so glad they didn't blend the words Ford and Fiat. I mean, who wants to be named Fat? Or Chevy and Jeep. Cheep Pierce? Bentley and Hummer would have made me a Bummer. So, I'll stick with Chonda. Although people who have heard me talk say Rambler fits perfectly.

You might think there were two middles in our family, but Mike seemed so grown up and so much older, that I was really the middle of three girls who often shared one bedroom (if the parsonage was big enough, only Cheralyn and I had to share a room.) Charlotta was beautiful and talented, and Cheralyn was the sweetest baby, so everybody just loved her. I was the runt, shorter and stubbier than my sisters, which meant the only way I could get a little attention was to cut up, act out, and be louder and bolder. I bet if you look at comedians, a vast majority of them are middle kids. (I bet if you look at bank robbers, circus clowns, and pole dancers, a vast majority of them are also middle kids.)

I looked up to Mike more than anyone; he was my Superman. My sisters played with dolls together while I followed Mike around everywhere, mostly to play putt-putt golf and basketball. Whenever we played a game, whether Monopoly, croquet, or badminton, it was the girls versus Mike and me, which put me officially in the running to be the most annoying tomboy little sister of all time. When we moved from South Carolina to Tennessee before my sophomore year in high school, I rode in the vehicle with my big brother who had come home from college in Nashville to help us move.

Moses and the Jews leaving Egypt had nothing on us when we made the trek. Remember that scene from *The Ten Commandments* movie with that caravan of the Jewish people and their animals? That was us, minus the parting of the Red Sea. Dad drove a U-Haul truck. Charlotta drove a car packed with all our clothes. Mom drove a car with Cheralyn and all our dishes. I rode in the church passenger van with Mike. And of course, we had to take out the seats and tie them to the top of the van so we could fit me, our cat, dog, and Shetland pony in the back. It was a drive of 577.8 miles to Tennessee, and I made it about half a mile until the smell from the animals got too overpowering. Then I climbed up into the passenger seat next to Mike.

Why did we leave South Carolina? That is something I asked myself over and over as a teenager. Honestly, we kids had little say about any move we ever made. Our parents would just sit us down and give us a story about a new "calling from God." Funny how God never called us to a giant church in Maui. Maybe the reason for moving was because it was always best to leave before the church people chased us out of town. And then there was that *other* dad. It would be many years later before my mother told me who Dad really was. A man with a terrible illness. A man in great need of medicine, intervention, and therapy. He never got it. My mother said to me, "Your father was diagnosed many years ago as 'manic-depressive borderline schizophrenic.'" I'm not sure I would have understood that as a kid. But I'm pretty sure it would have been better than the words I used to describe my dad through the years.

I have specific memories of what that means and how his mental state affected me and others, as well as sights, sounds, and scenes embedded so deeply in my mind that that no one can tell me they didn't happen.

Some people would say it's *my truth.* I've always resented when people say, "Well, that's your truth." It sounds like they're saying what I remember may not have happened in reality. They're saying what I and others experienced and how those things molded me was all based on my poor memory.

Nevertheless, I can't remember a church, a town, or a move that didn't include the whispers about my dad and his infidelity. My father had a girlfriend in every church. And on the rare occasions he was not having an affair with one of the local ladies, he was locked away in his room under a heap of deep, suicidal depression. Yet somehow, between being sequestered in his own bedroom or infiltrating someone else's, he pastored. Ironically, most parishioners would testify as to how wonderful he was—a great teacher and compassionate preacher, consoling them during times of grief and counseling them through the ups and downs of their lives. He always went the extra mile for everyone except his family. People would swear Pastor Courtney was the best pastor they ever had, and they would be correct. Their truth is as true as mine. You can be two things at once, and that's what he was—a good pastor and a horrible father.

If you think our political elections were tense in 2020, here is how it worked in our church on "election Sunday" back in the day. The members of each congregation voted every year on whether to keep the pastor. Keeping my dad meant we had a place to live (no matter how small), food (no matter how much government cheese and butter we needed), and a van. The prospect of being voted out was the scariest thing ever. I don't know why the church did it that way. It's a horrible event for a pastor, his wife, and their kids.

On "election Sunday," our whole family would stand at the front of the church while the congregation marched past us. We would shake hands with the parishioners and get lots of hugs, except from the "No" voters. They'd usually stay in their seats and avoid eye contact all together. (I've often joked that I was the only one with the nerve to hold up a sign saying, "Vote No. We don't like you either.")

My dad was smart enough to anticipate whether he was about to be voted out or not. If he sensed they were going to run him out of town, he would line up a new church in another town before they asked him to leave.

I was fifteen when we made that 577.8-mile trek from South Carolina to Ashland City, Tennessee. It would be the last move we ever made as a family. What a culture shock. We went from sandals to cowboy boots, from sand dunes to the rolling hills of middle Tennessee. No sidewalks. No beach. No McDonald's. And no more pretending everything was okay at home.

I first became aware of the problems my parents had when I and probably half the neighbors heard them having a huge fight. It wasn't just the 120 decibels that affected me; it was hearing the name of a certain woman being tossed around. The lady had children, and Mom seemed especially sickened by that. She kept saying over and over, "You have three precious girls in the next room. How do you think they will feel when they find out what you've been doing?"

After Mike went away to college, I became Dad's "right hand man." I held the flashlight when he changed the oil and steadied the bottom of the ladder while he fixed a hole in the roof, and he often took me with him to call on parishioners.

One such visit was to a military wife while her husband was stationed in another country, defending our freedom. Dad said he had promised to "look in on her" and told me to wait in the car and do my homework while he *ministered*. I finished my Algebra and English assignments and waited for what seemed like hours. By then I needed to go to the potty. Really bad, too. When I couldn't wait any longer, I got out of the car and knocked on the door of the double-wide. No answer. My bladder was reaching its breaking point, so I opened the door carefully and stepped inside. The military wife came shuffling out of the bedroom toward me, her hair a mess, and my dad came barreling down the hall right behind her. "I told you to wait in the car!" he hissed. I was still a bit naïve, so I didn't understand why the lady needed to be ministered to in her bedroom.

Another time, Mom couldn't get an answer on Dad's office phone. Supper was getting cold, so she told me to head over to the church to tell him dinner was on the table. I loved any excuse to drive my little motorbike, so I putt-putted down the three blocks to the church. I went to the study and opened the door without knocking and simultaneously turned on the light while yelling, "Supper's ready!"

What's the smallest measure of time? A nanosecond? Well, in that nanosecond, I caught a glimpse of Dad and one of the church ladies doing something specifically banned by about half the states back in 1975, and then I saw my dad flying toward me. With his belt in his hand. I guess it had already been unbuckled for a while by then.

I tried to reach my bike as fast as possible, but as quick as I was, Dad and his belt were quicker. With each slap of leather and metal as he whipped my back, I could hear him say. "Don't. (*whip*) You. (*whip*) Ever. (*whip*) Come into my office again without knocking!" *Whip, whip, whip.*

I then realized what Mom had known all along. If the belt and Dad's infidelity hurt me, it hurt Mom ten times more. It was just before my eighteenth birthday that Dad finally left for good. That was also the time I finally drew a line. I decided I would never again go quietly into the night. Okay, maybe that was a bit dramatic. But I do think that I simply decided I would never again cover for him, excuse him, or trust him. No matter how painful the consequences physically or emotionally—I would stand up to him. And I did.

## CHAPTER 2

# FAMILY SECRETS

Some memories remain very hard for me to reveal. How I wish I had a different story to tell. So, sit back, breathe deep, and please understand why I made the decision to share this. Believe me, this story has been filtered through a myriad of counseling appointments, conversations, and prayers. Lots of prayers.

I don't think anyone wants to reveal the most terrible details about themselves. There is no trophy for living the toughest life on earth. At least, I don't think there is. If there is, I could come closer to winning that trophy than an Oscar. No, this story is only told because of you. Someone reading this has walked a similar road. You may have taken a long time to come to terms with your own story. Trust me on this, find a private audience before you go public. Find someone to help you unravel what has been twisted inside you for a lifetime. Yes, this story is not just for me, but for many others.

To say it directly with no softening language, my dad was abusive. Period. And in a myriad of ways. I kept it secret from so many people for decades.

Why did I keep it secret? The same reason many kids keep that sort of thing buried deep within themselves. When you're a little kid, you don't want to break up your family. Plus, who would believe a child speaking out against a man of the cloth? He was a pastor, a role model for his flock. If no one believed me, I would have been the devil child...and if they did believe me, then Dad would have lost his job, and we would have been homeless and starved.

Most people can remember with great fondness the Christmas they got their first bicycle, their favorite family vacation, when they found out about Santa Claus. I have giant gaps in my brain with very few of those memories. But there are things that did happen, things that were hidden, blurred deliberately, that later in my life became all too real and clear.

I was sitting in a rehab facility for depression in Scottsdale, Arizona, when a forty-something adult woman turned to me and said, "So, your father molested you?"

I immediately said, "Oh, no, he didn't touch me. I was his buddy." It was the first time I heard my own voice tell this story out loud.

My first memory of it was probably the harshest. I was around ten or eleven years old. He was sitting in his recliner in our Myrtle Beach living room in his tighty-whities. My mom was in the kitchen, just a few feet away, washing dishes. Dad called me over and slid his arm around my waist. A Bible rested on one knee; a small handgun balanced on the other. I called out for my mom, but all I heard was, "I'll be right there in a minute." Dad's hand was down his underpants. I decided to stare at the gun.

Those images were buried inside my memory for many years until a moment in group therapy in Scottsdale brought them to the surface. As I blurted out the details to my counselor, many in the group began to cry. Others were indifferent—not because they were callous—but because if you were in that group, chances are your story was just as bad or even worse. In the process, I learned that sexual abuse did not have to include being touched.

Our instruction that particular day was to act out a memory. The idea was that, in acting it out, we would release what had been stuck and hidden, and we would flesh out details that had been repressed. If it worked, memories would start to flow freely (think of it as unclogging a drain).

As I got ready to act out moments from my past, an older man volunteered to play the part of my dad. The therapist provided a box of props to symbolize different characters in the story: a doll for Cheralyn, who was playing in her room down the hall; a hand mirror for Charlotta, because she was always fixing her long hair; an apron for Mom in the kitchen—nearby yet so far away from being able to help. My brother had just left for college during this incident, but I still symbolize him by choosing a tall guy in the corner and asked him to wear a red cape around his shoulders while standing outside the scene. Mike, my Superman, but this time he wasn't able to save Lois Lane.

We placed the dad's chair in the middle of our circle. I can still recall every detail of my father's chair. The green vinyl arm rests. The way it creaked as you pushed it back to recline. The metal hinges that would pinch your fingers if you stood too close when it folded upward. Seeing the man playing my dad there, sitting in a green vinyl chair just like the one in the living room of our house in Myrtle Beach, opened up that locked-away part of my brain. A torrent of emotion hit me, and the power of it broke open the vault to my secrets. It all came spewing out...all of it.

After completely exhausting everyone in the room with my blubbering sobs, I did what a comedian always does in times of stress. A joke formed in my brain, one with a punchline about which would go off first, the gun or my dad. (I realize that was crass, but bear with me for a moment.) Saying something funny and edgy in the moment is exactly what I've done for years... but not on that day. The joke died within me. And something was born in its wake—a resolve to let the pain of this abuse and the fight that it took to face it head on point the way for others to find healing.

Could I have gone to the church to get help when I was eleven? Fifty-plus years ago, even if I had been mature enough to decide to seek help, there was nowhere to go, no one to talk to. There was no #MeToo, no #TimesUp, no 1-800 number for a little girl like me to call. Tragically, a half century later, too few women and children in my situation feel they have someone to hear their stories. Even if they are heard, they are not really listened to.

I was alone. But not anymore.

I have since discovered I have so many brothers and sisters in the world who were sexually abused. The focus for several years was on predatory priests, but if you google the words "pastor" and "sexual abuse," you'll see countless articles. Look up the latest scandals involving Southern Baptists. It's an epidemic in every religious denomination, and our collective silence empowers these sick individuals to prey on their own and other people's kids. They use their position of authority from the pulpit or as parents in the same twisted way as a Hollywood movie executive. And as with the perverts in Hollywood, these abusers' time is up. Their crimes are being exposed.

My friend Anne Beiler of Auntie Anne's Pretzels has written several books about events in her life. On several occasions, I have listened to Anne tell her darkest story of "the abuse of spiritual power." She said, "I am all too familiar with the smothering darkness that comes with bearing secrets. I don't want to waste a single moment of my pain. And my passage from despair to freedom in no way meant my life became pain-free. Sometimes healing feels like ripping off a scab and then pouring salt water into the wound. Sometimes a memory is triggered without warning and takes me back forty years to painful moments that altered my life forever."[1]

That's why, as painful as my experience was, I share it to let those who have also endured this trauma know that you are not alone. I wanted to turn my mess into a message. Like me, you can do more than simply survive. And it starts with talking about the proverbial elephant in the room.

Side note: A *trigger* refers to something that affects your emotional state, often significantly, by causing extreme distress. If this has triggered you in anyway, put this book down and call a friend. Better yet, call a Christian counselor who will help you get the secrets and lies woven within you *out.*

I've often wondered how my mom dealt with it. How did she endure the heartache of living with my father's infidelity? How did she survive his abuse, his tantrums, the humiliation as a woman?

When my dad was in one of his dark moods, it was traumatic for our whole family. I'm not sure what was worse, his intense, angry outbursts or his depression. At times, he was so depressed, we would hear him weeping so mournfully that we'd rush out of our rooms to see what the matter was. He would pause, waving his gun, his hair a mess, then look up at us and mumble, "Don't be scared when you hear a loud noise because I'm going to kill myself tonight."

Once I mustered the courage to stare him down and say, "Good luck, Dad. You've been trying this for years." He froze, tossed the gun onto the couch, then stomped into his bedroom and slammed the door. And strangely, my mom just said, "Well, thank you, honey, for

1 Anne Beiler, *The Secret Lies Within: An Inside Out Look at Overcoming Trauma and Finding Purpose in the Pain* (New York: Morgan James Publishing, 2020), 3.

whatever you said to Daddy. Now, let's all go to bed," as if we had just finished a bedtime story.

It's common to think of soldiers in conjunction with PTSD, however, I have learned it can be caused by neglect and abuse as well as by experiencing or witnessing extraordinary events. Some of the sights and sounds and scenes from that part of my life still crop up in my mind. Dishes shattering against the kitchen walls. My brother sleeping with a knife under his pillow. I clearly remember my brother wrestling on the floor to take the gun out of our dad's hands. As they wrestled to the floor, Mom rushed me and my sisters out of the house and drove us to my cousin's house. I felt so relieved the next day when I learned Mike was okay. He and Dad had worn each other out and fallen asleep before any shots were fired. Ask Mike about this today—he has little recollection. Yet, I remember this vividly.

I was furious for so long about what my dad put all of us through and why everyone was powerless to stop it. But as the dust settled over the years, I gained great compassion for my mom. Yes, she could have handled things differently. And then years after *all* of this, I inherited the very thing I despised about my father. Mental illness. I was diagnosed with clinical depression. And I'm pretty sure I inherited a vast ability to compartmentalize from my mother. She had an uncanny way of standing in the tsunami and collecting seashells, oblivious to the crash just ahead. That gift from her would later be a blessing *and* a curse.

I was angry, and I needed help. I held so much inside, but occasionally, like steam escaping, it would leak out. Weeks after I left rehab in Arizona in 2001, my brother listened as I recounted the events of my stay. I burst into uncontrollable sobs as we knelt at the couch crying aloud to God, "Why? Why did we have to go through all that?"

But "why?" is an unanswerable question, and knowing the answer wouldn't have changed the past. One can't un-ring a bell, and I can't undo what my father did. Instead, I have learned to turn that anger into a passion for being there to help others. And that's why Mike and I determined we would one day open a recovery center that offers counseling and treatment to those with depression, anxiety, and addiction, regardless of their ability to pay.[2] And we did. More on that later.

2 Branches, www.branches.org.

## CHAPTER 3

# FIRST LOVES AND FIRST LOSSES

After we moved to Ashland City, I entered my sophomore year of high school. The future looked promising at first. Dad began pastoring a new church; Mom had—in her mind at least—maybe, just maybe, left her tears behind in South Carolina; Mike and Charlotta were in college only forty miles away; and I fell in love for the first time.

His name was Butch, and he looked exactly as you might picture a teenager named Butch in 1975—tall, skinny, and gap-toothed, with red hair. What was I thinking? If Archie and Jughead had a son, he would look like Butch. (Obviously, if they had a son, it would be a scientific miracle.) Butch and I had a deep, abiding love, the purest love ever. We were the Tennessee version of Romeo and Juliet, if Shakespeare had named his main characters Butch and Chonda. (Somehow, I get the feeling that would not have been the big seller that *Romeo and Juliet* ended up being.) But there were no two teenagers more in love than we were. Butch liked politics and so did I. When the other girls in school were reading *Vogue* to check out the latest fashions, I was reading the *New York Times* and *Time*. We were perfect for each other. We were both fifteen, and our romance lasted about six months, but the heartbreak? Well, that has lasted about forty years!

Our little fling that summer was a secret to most. We had a mutual friend named Dale who would take me to meet up with Butch, since under Dad Rule number 1757.6 I was not allowed to be in a car with a boy. I guess it never dawned on anyone that Dale was a boy. But he was older and in college, and my mother adored him and trusted him completely. I think it was also Dale who eventually broke the news to me that while I was home pining away for my next little secret kiss with Butch, Butch was staying busy with every other girl around town.

That was my first heartbreak. I was devastated. I mean, my heart was not only broken, but was crushed, shattered, and swept away on a Tennessee breeze. The fact that we were supposed to keep our relationship a secret, well, that probably should have been my first clue that it would never last. Butch wasn't helping me keep a secret from my parents; he was keeping *me* a secret from Betty Jo, Denise, Cindy, and half the cheerleading squad. And since I was an expert at keeping secrets by then, I should have seen through his. But our romance was over, and my broken heart was as real as it gets for a fifteen-year-old girl.

Usually, it was Mike who helped me deal with life's setbacks, but this time it was my sister Charlotta who consoled me with a poem she wrote. It's too long to quote in its entirety, but reading the first stanza put me in a better mood immediately.

> You're beautiful, little sister
> Your eyes so big and blue
> Sparkle as you tell the world
> How Jesus makes life new

Butch and I had a mutual best friend David (yes, my future husband David). They had taken a poor-man's senior trip to Colorado in a beat-up VW Beetle. They camped and fished, and what I was told later was there was a lot of Chonda talk between the two of them! Butch wanted to let me know he was pursuing a political career, attending college in Washington, D.C., and interning for a congressman.

For a little bit, I thought of myself as crackerjack First Lady material. Now? I think of me as a First Lady and crack-up. My diplomacy would probably cause a war. Plus, if Butch had turned out like Bill Clinton, the White House may not be standing. And in case you're not a history or political science major, Butch never became president. It's hard to imagine the inauguration of a President Butch, and I would never mention the fact that although things didn't work out for him, they did for me. I run into Butch occasionally. We smile. We are friendly. We have a few laughs. But, deep down, I think any woman (or man) who was dumped can connect with Toby Keith's song "How Do You Like Me Now?!"

Oh, come on. I can't be the only woman who has looked for tiny ways to get back at the boy who broke her heart. It could have been worse for Butch. I could be Carrie Underwood singing that song about using my key to scratch up his fancy car and taking out the headlights with a baseball bat. And even scarier, I could be Taylor Swift. You're not a boy she dates; you're the first words in her next "I Hate You" song.

My post-Butch love life can be summed up in Ariana Grande's song "Thank U, Next." For next after Butch was Kevin. Kevin lasted a bit longer than Butch. Then there were Matthew, Mark, Luke, and John. (No, not the ones from the Bible. I'm not that old.) There was also a Jake, a Ted, and representatives from the rest of the alphabet. I looked for love under every rock in the county until I got distracted by an actual deep, abiding, real love—the theater.

I joined the drama department at Cheatham County High. For a girl who came from a poor background and had been forced to move so many times, I found acceptance on that high school stage, a kind of family with my fellow thespians (and that is not a dirty word). The stage became my home.

When I wasn't in class or on the school stage, I was working. We didn't have a choice. Pastors in Ashland County aren't exactly on the Forbes 400 list. Maybe on the $400-in-the-bank-account list. So I got a part-time job at Shirley's Bakery as a waitress during the breakfast shift from 5:30 to 7:30 in the morning. When I finished delivering the #2 breakfast special (eggs, bacon, toast, and coffee for $2.99) to the local clientele, I headed to school on my motorcycle. After class I'd work the dinner crowd shift until 6:30. It was very exciting, and the best part was that it involved my first brush with an actual show business legend: Miss Tanya Tucker! She came in one night and ordered a bowl of beans and cornbread. She drove a jeep. She was only two years older than me and was already a superstar, but even then, I could see the comparisons. We were like peas in a pod. We both were blonde, we both could sing "Delta Dawn," and we both liked beans and cornbread. It might have been the first time I could envision something different than staying in Ashland City all my life.

After the dinner shift was over, I'd head home to do my schoolwork and spend some time with my new friend, David.

David had such a sad story. His dad was an alcoholic, and the two of them often slept in the concession stand at the park because they had no place to live. Every month when his dad's VA check would come, there'd be a race to the mailbox to see who would get it first. If David got it, they'd have groceries and rent money for a month. If his dad got it, he'd drink it all up, spend the night in jail, and David would end up sleeping in the concession stand alone. Mom felt sorry for David, so she'd let him sleep on our couch (until she noticed we were being flirty with each other, then he had to go back to the concession stand).

David was a nice guy, a champion wrestler, good-looking, and smart, and he became such a good friend that a couple years later, I married him. But before that, I began to feel some breathing room in my life. My dad started avoiding me after I stood up to him several times. I loved drama class, had a lot of boyfriends, and had a wonderful friend in David. Then my world started to fall apart.

It was the day before the bicentennial, July 3, 1976. Charlotta left the house early for work because there was a rainstorm. The roads were slippery, but she had driven that same wet road a hundred times; we all had, so it was no big deal.

But that day was different, and within a few hours, the call came. Charlotta's car had hydroplaned into the path of an oncoming vehicle, and she was hit on the driver's side. Her life was over in an instant. My beloved older sister, one of God's angels on Earth, was now an angel in Heaven. She was only twenty years old.

It didn't feel real at all. Within hours, our house was full of people, coming as people do in times like that, bringing food and words of comfort. I kept answering the door, hoping that maybe it was all a mistake, and she would be there. It was all so strange. Surely somehow, someone could make it all better.

Then the door opened, and my brother Mike walked in. Mike could fix anything. He was my Superman, the rock of the family, and I was sure he would bring Charlotta back. He always made everything right. He walked over to me and hugged me, and then I knew. Charlotta was gone, and my life and our family would never be the same.

It's been more than forty years, and I still think about her every day. On July 3, 2006, I posted this about the day that changed us forever:

> This was like any other day. I was sixteen and went to my morning part-time job at my cousin's insurance office. Did a little filing, answered a few phone calls. Then, my little sister called and said, "Dad called, and he is getting Mom at the hairdresser's. He said lock the office and be outside. A policeman came by to take him and Mom to the hospital in Nashville. Something has happened."
>
> My parents dropped me off at the corner and I walked the rest of the way home. Cheralyn was on the porch. We sat huddled for a bit. We had just sat at the breakfast table with Charlotta that morning. I decided to call Sears, where Charlotta worked in Nashville.
>
> "She will know what's going on," I told Cheralyn. The lady on the switchboard said, "Honey, we've been wondering about Charlotta. She didn't come in yet this morning."
>
> My heart sank. Somehow, I knew. I just knew. I sat on the piano bench and tinkered around on the keys. A songbook laid open to the song Charlotta had practiced and sang the Wednesday night before:
>
> Take the dearest things to me, if that's how it must be
> To draw me closer to thee
> Leave this world far behind—
> There are new heights to climb . . .
> If through sorrow more like You I become.
>
> Then the phone rang. My dad's voice cracked. Before he could stumble through the words I simply said, "I know,

Dad. You'll have to tell Cheralyn." I handed her the phone and watched her melt into the loudest scream, "No. Pleeeease, NO! My Sissy. My Sissy."

Charlotta Kay Courtney
Born May 10th, 1956
Died July 3rd, 1976
I love you and miss you still . . .

My faith in God was not shattered, but it sure was starting to show some cracks. We're told there is a reason for everything, but for the life of me, I couldn't see why this happened. Mom was devastated. Mike and I were crushed, Cheralyn was a lost soul. My parents' marriage was hanging by a thread to say the least. I think grieving Charlotta more than likely obliterated that tiny strand, and in November the following year, Dad left.

Let me point out that this is not the response you see from TV sitcom fathers. That is not the reaction advised in the "How to Be a Dad Handbook."

Time and time again, Dad had threatened to leave Mom, but this time he really did. Of course, he had to wait until the timing was right, which meant leaving just when the family needed him most. So he officiated at my brother's wedding, waited until Mike and his new wife, Doris, drove off for their honeymoon, then packed up and left. In my Datsun. Let me make that 100 percent clear. He drove away in the Datsun I had worked so hard to buy. *In my car!* My dad literally stole my car.

Let's put that in perspective. Some dads borrow cars. Other dads will sometimes ask you for a lift. My friend Jones bought his daughter's old truck so she would have money for a new one, but he didn't steal it. Have you ever heard of a dad stealing his daughter's car? That has got to go into *Ripley's Believe It or Not: Dysfunctional*

*Family Edition.* And the sad part is, he was so bad for us, so bad for my mom, that I was more angry about him leaving in my car than about the fact that he left us. Truth is, it's hard to leave when you're really not there.

As Dad was driving away—in my Datsun that he stole—Mom called Mike and Doris. Not on a cellphone, mind you, since this was in the days of landlines, telegrams, and Pony Express. She called the hotel where they had honeymoon reservations. After hearing the message, they turned right around and came home to help Mom and eventually moved on to start their own life together. Even after he filed for divorce, Dad would occasionally call to tell Mom he was ready to come home, but she had reached the point where she couldn't deal with him anymore. I can understand why. Living with a man with whom she shared so many secrets was too hard on her.

In many ways, Dad's leaving was liberating for Mom. She started to come into her own, and our house became the hangout for half the teenagers in town. I'd come home from school to find my classmates watching TV and eating snacks. They even called my mom "Mrs. C" for Mrs. Courtney, the same way the Fonz called Mrs. Cunningham "Mrs. C." She was enjoying her newfound freedom. Cooking and cleaning for all those teenagers and being their den mother enabled her to deal with my dad's skipping town.

So, it was me and Mom and Cheralyn, a daytime house full of teenagers...and David. David and I dated off and on from the time I was sixteen—more off than on. We were more like best friends. Our high school graduation ceremony was held at the church, and afterward, the two of us sat on the front steps. David was unusually quiet. Suddenly, he buried his head in his hands. "What's the matter, Ace?" I asked. (Ace was his nickname.)

"Something horrible has happened," he said. "I think I've fallen in love with you."

Well, thanks a lot, Ace. There is nothing more romantic than telling a young woman that being in love with her is horrible. Why not throw in that her nose is too big, her butt is too flat, and she's a bad kisser. I made it clear to David that he and I were just friends, and I didn't want him to interfere with my quest to set the Tennessee record for getting marriage proposals. (I think I still have the record; you can check it in the Cheatham County Courthouse. Rumor is they even have a plaque.)

"Most marriage proposals to a girl under age eighteen, Chonda Courtney: 37 proposals by her senior year of high school."

Remember, it's Tennessee. Back then, if you weren't married by the time you turned nineteen, you were a spinster. Heck, some girls back then got so desperate, they married outside the family. (I will now pause while the Tennessee Chamber of Commerce sends me an angry email.)

I don't know why this was so, but during my young adult years, guys kept asking me to marry them. I got more marriage proposals than a season of all the Kardashians put together. And my answer was always no. Maybe because deep down I realized David and I were soulmates. But it was also because any kind of intimacy scared me to death. When you lose your big sister and your father, you get scared of any close human connection. I was perfectly happy with my family being me and mom and Cheralyn—until one day, Cheralyn got sick.

I was a senior in high school and was helping to keep us afloat by working as a nurse's aide from 11:00 p.m. to 7:00 a.m. while also holding a part-time day job filing things in my cousin's insurance business. When I say filing "things," I mean that literally. I had no idea what I was filing, but I was pretty accurate at making sure everything got into the right folder in the right drawer. (My apologies if for some reason you had a relative who had a claim denied in Ashland City, Tennessee, in 1978 because of lost "things." It might have been my fault.) In addition to working two jobs and going to class, I was also in the school choir. Cheralyn and I were in the school musical *Oklahoma!* She had a ballet solo, and being a senior, I performed the lead role of Laurey.

For the first time in two years, we were having fun instead of sitting around crying over Charlotta. On Saturday night, the final performance of the musical, we should have been excited, but Cheralyn kept saying she wasn't feeling well. She missed church the next day, and by Monday she had spiked a high fever. The doctor thought it was mono, so we took her to the hospital to get some blood work done. As we waited for the results, a strange feeling crept over me—the same feeling I had when the phone rang with the call about Charlotta's accident.

I got up from the waiting room to ask if I could see my sister, but the nurse told me she was in isolation. That was odd. Why would they do that with mono? Maybe so we wouldn't catch it? Then I thought it through. With mono, your immune system is weak, so they must not want *her* to catch a cold from *us*. I was sorting through my thoughts and trying to figure out what was going on when two doctors asked to talk to Mom. Alone. Without me. Strange.

As I watched them in conversation across the room, I saw Mom's shoulders slump. I felt a chill. Something was wrong, horribly wrong. They ushered me and Mom out of the crowded waiting room into a little side room and broke the news.

"Cheralyn doesn't have mono, and it isn't the flu. Cheralyn has leukemia." My heart sank.

I asked the doctor point-blank, "Is she going to die?"

"More than likely, she will," his answer rang in my ear.

The news affected us all so deeply. My brother Mike did what he always tried to do—flip a switch and go into his "fix-it" mode. Like so many times throughout my childhood, he was determined to be the one to save the day. So when we discovered Mike was an exact match for a bone marrow transplant for Cheralyn, it didn't surprise me a bit that he wanted to donate it to her. He had convinced himself his bone marrow would miraculously heal her; and not only that, but he had also somehow talked himself into the idea that once she was healed, it would snap Dad to his senses, and we would all be a family again. Two miracles would occur.

My dad had parked an RV in the hospital parking lot so he could visit from time to time. He had a "friend" there with him. I loathed him walking into Cheralyn's room. I stood at her bedside, seething with anger boiling up inside me every time he reached for Cheralyn's hand or tried to stroke her hair. And Mom? Wow, I look back and for the life of me cannot understand how she maintained any strength at all. The other woman was parked outside the door, and my father was crying and mumbling like he was some victim of it all while Cheralyn slowly slipped away.

Late on a Friday evening, Cheralyn was put into intensive care. She had contracted pneumonia as they assaulted the cancer with the harshest chemotherapy available. It was torture seeing her suffer. She would hallucinate due to the morphine they gave her for pain, her hair fell out in giant clumps, and the sores around her mouth and down her throat blistered and broke. It was a grueling three weeks, but I thought maybe, just maybe, it was going to be over once they gave her Mike's bone marrow. The operation was scheduled for the following Monday, but they never started the transplant.

Cheralyn died on Saturday morning. Only twenty-one days passed from the time she was diagnosed until she left us on May 13, 1978. My little sister was gone.

## CHAPTER 4

# COLLEGE AND A GOD ENCOUNTER

I stared at the medicine vials and bandages strewn across the counter in Cheralyn's small treatment room. None of it had kept my sister alive. Rage welled up from somewhere inside me, and without thinking, I raked my arm across the counter, knocking everything onto the floor. I think I screamed. At least I know I wanted to. My mother wrapped her arms around my shoulders. The doctor mumbled something about giving me a sedative, but Mom calmly said, "Give her a minute. She'll be fine."

Mike went home with Doris, and I went home with family friends, the Lockerts. I snuggled on the bed with my dearest friend, Julie Lockert. She stroked my head and whispered as I sobbed, "It's okay, let it all out." Mother had camped out in Cheralyn's room nonstop. We were all exhausted, heartbroken. We had very little money, there was no allowance from the church, and we felt like outcasts, as one can only be when a preacher has deserted his family in a small Southern town.

Over the months that followed, Dad would write or call Mom and talk to her about coming back home. I would tell her again and again, "No! If he comes back, I'm leaving." It was a hard thing to say, but I knew Mom didn't want to lose another daughter. It was especially hard when we were struggling financially or on the nights when Mom would fall apart, broken and lonely. But I was fed up with the cycle. Dad had lost the right to use us and abuse us.

I tried to do what I could to help. I attended high school on weekdays and still worked the night shift to help pay for groceries, and the hospital bills, and the mortgage, but there was no amount of work or pay that would allow us to keep up with the bills. We had to sell the house.

I've never been one to be sentimental about material things. It would be many years before I would come to understand the pain it must have caused my mother to have to move from her home after twenty-five years of marriage and raising four kids. Her family of six was reduced to the two of us, and now her cherished keepsakes and memories of two dead daughters and gifts from a man who broke her heart again and again all wound up displayed across tables in one big yard sale.

That was my idea. Rather than pay to move things we couldn't keep anyway, I figured we'd pick up some money by having a sale. It sounded like a brilliant idea at the time. Trouble was, we lived at the top of a steep hill, and we were worried no one would want to walk up to see what we had. Then I had an even more brilliant idea. In fact, it was pure genius for me. I would lure people up the hill by dressing as Raggedy Ann and waving my arms wildly at cars until people stopped to see what the crazy girl was up to, then I'd direct them up the street to the house. (You know those air-filled, waving-arm inflatables outside stores, or the real estate guys on the corner spinning their signs? I was the 1978 version of that.)

It worked. People came in droves. They thought they were buying furniture and knick-knacks, but that's not true. They were buying our memories—my memories—of a time when Mike was home, my sisters were alive, and we were a family. A dysfunctional family, but still, a family.

Once the sale was over and the house was sold, Mom and I moved about thirty miles away to Nashville into a one-bedroom apartment in a senior living complex across from Trevecca Nazarene College, where I was enrolled in classes. Let me repeat that. We moved into a senior citizens' home. Not the ones you see on TV ads, which look like some combination of a Caribbean resort and a country club. I mean a real senior citizens' home—with old people shuffling about with walkers and mumbling about their lost cats. Think about it, I was a teenager in an old folks' home. Sounds like the title of a horror movie, doesn't it? "She was trapped with no hope of escape. More horrifying than *Jaws* and *A Quiet Place*, it's *Teenager in an Old Folks' Home*."

And the worst part: we were living there quasi-illegally because you were supposed to be a senior to have an apartment there. Even Mom was way too young, but the man who ran it was very gracious and let us move in.

If you're a mom and you want your daughter to stay pure and chaste, the best thing to do is have her live with you in a one-bedroom apartment in a senior citizens' home. Mom in a bed ten feet away, the smell of Vicks VapoRub permeating the place, and walkers double-parked in the hallway is better than any abstinence program ever invented. Throw in a pair of pantyhose as a chastity belt, and I was destined to be purer than an eighty-year-old spinster aunt. And to make triple-y sure that I'd remember how concerned my mom was about my innocence, she would pray out loud for me—while we were laying in the same bed! Did you ever meet anyone who would confess your sins to the Lord *for* you? That was my mother. She must have wanted to save me the trouble.

"Oh, Lord, please forgive Chonda for her sins." Then she would turn to me. "Honey, what did you do wrong today?"

"Nothing, leave me alone."

"Oh, Lord, forgive her for talking back to her mother, for looking at a boy with lust, and for not taking out the trash."

I'm pretty sure I heard the Lord laugh and say, "I got it. But trust me, Mom, she's a tough one."

The best part was when we'd have a fight and Mom would get mad at me. She'd say, "Go to your room," and I'd say, "This is my room!"

Thankfully, there was one large walk-in closet in that apartment. I often pulled a chair into it to sit and read. I wanted to feel like I had my own space. When I was ready to talk, I'd come out of the closet. (To be clear, I was in *a* closet, not *the* closet.)

I had no idea what typical eighteen-year-old girls were doing the summer before college. I worked at night as a nurse's aide with my mom. I slept during the day, woke up to eat something, saw David when I could, and walked to work across the parking lot from our new place. David and I would occasionally take the long drive to the cemetery. I visited my two sisters there, and he would sit by me. Neither of us spoke much as we sat and pulled weeds there, simply trying to keep breathing.

Working so many hours while trying to go to school meant my grades were not great. It reminds me of the college football player who brought home his first report card with four Fs and a D, and his dad said, "I see your problem. You're concentrating too much on one subject."

My mother's brother, Uncle Gerald, paid for my first year of college. Trevecca Nazarene College was expensive.

I was probably in no frame of mind to be a serious student (kind of like Lori Loughlin's kid). And I was not in the frame of mind to be a student where they actually locked you in at night. Remember, I was a rebel! Albeit a rebel with a conscience that I argued with often.

"Rules and regulations? That's suppression, not protection. Rules are made to be broken."

"What? That's not what you were taught, Chonda."

"Yeah, Conscience, but we all know well-behaved women seldom make history."

That was the dialogue going on in my mind when I was asked to leave school. A real shocker, I know. Yes, they asked me to leave college. What? Chonda's not a Mensa member? Okay, getting caught sneaking out of a dorm room didn't help. I still don't know why it was a problem—it wasn't my dorm room! Besides, I could see my mother's senior living apartment building from my window. It wasn't like I was sneaking out to see a guy. I was sneaking out *after* seeing a guy.

So, Trevecca and I mutually agreed that a new school would be best. Fortunately, I found another college that was perfect for me—Austin Peay State University in Clarksville, Tennessee. A little over an hour's drive from my mother's door. Not too far away, but far enough that I could have my own life away from the Vicks VapoRub and old people yet still go home to see Mom if she needed me.

Truth is, I needed her a whole lot more than she needed me. Deep inside where joy and fun and enthusiasm are supposed to reside in a twenty-year-old heart, I was empty. Oh, I stayed busy in the theater department; acting and singing were a wonderful distraction. But any class that required opening a textbook instead of opening my mouth? Well, they fell by the wayside. I stayed absorbed in the recent character I was playing on stage; but there is a cost to that, and I'm not talking about the D in Intro to English Lit 101. The cost is missing out on what some call the "God-shaped hole"—that inner connection that whispers to your spirit that there is something bigger and better. There is something out there, Someone out there who will soothe a troubled soul better than any drug, relationship, or career.

There is no empty like a "once was" empty. In other words, I once had exuberance to tell the world about Jesus. I kept Gospel tracts in my purse just in case someone needed the "Four Spiritual Laws"! If I could have played the guitar—I would have been just like Sean Feucht singing praise songs in the middle of the riots in Portland. But that "once was" space in my heart was hurt and empty—a "once was" empty. (I had walked down the aisle at church to *get saved* at the age of four, again at seven, twice when I was nine, and I can't even remember how many times in my teens.) But it was thanks to a call from Mom that I rekindled my relationship with the Lord in college, and I have a feeling that was exactly what she was hoping all the other times she called and asked me to come home for a visit. Some people say God came to them in a dream. Others, like Moses, found God in a burning bush. Me? I knew deep in my heart that there was an Almighty Supreme Being because He helped me survive owning and driving a Chevy Chevette. If you ever had a Chevette and are still alive today, you know God is real. I didn't have just any Chevette. When I was at Austin Peay, I owned and drove the *world's worst Chevette.*

I'll never forget it. Mother was worried about me being away at Austin Peay, and she wanted me to come home on weekends. She always knew when I was up to no good. It was usually on a day that ended with a *y*. You know the Tom Cruise movie *Minority Report* where police utilize psychic technology to catch people before they commit their crimes? I swear Mom was the inspiration for that.

It started the way all her long-distance interrogation scenes did, with her asking me on the phone how things were between me and the Lord. Then she would test me by surprising me with a pop quiz and ask me to recite a Bible verse. I would always say "Jesus wept."

That day, my two-word answer didn't convince her, so she demanded I come home and go to church with her. And being an obedient daughter, I got in my Chevette, which is a French word for "tin can on wheels."

Let me paint a picture of this alleged car as best as I can. The Chevette is to cars what a pork chop on a stick is to a steak at the Palm; it's Chonda Pierce compared to Jennifer Aniston; it's what the Miami Dolphins are to a real football team. (My publisher just cringed and said that line will hurt book sales in Miami, but Dolphin fans would have to buy this book to know I said it, so I bet we didn't lose any sales.)

The Chevette had an AM radio but no air conditioning or heat. I lost the gear shift knob, so I stuck a potato on it to keep from cutting my hand. On a hot day I could smell French fries. At least the windshield wipers worked . . . Oops, that's not true. The wiper, singular, lonelier than a Donald Trump supporter in a MAGA hat at an Alexandra Ocasio-Cortez rally in New York City, would work once every three months for no apparent reason. The only thing that would prevent it from randomly beginning to work was if it was raining because—and this is a little-known fact but is scientifically accurate—the wipers on a Chevette were allergic to rain. You couldn't touch the passenger door because if you tried to open it, the window would fall down the track into the door itself and rattle. My solution: I put a "do not disturb" sign on the door and sealed it with duct tape.

It gets worse. I couldn't get in the car through the driver's side because the door had fallen off one day. My even more amazing solution was to wire the door shut and climb in and out of the car through the hatchback. That was not easy to do in a dress. The last thing a churchgoing girl like me wanted to do was reenact Sharon Stone's scene from *Basic Instinct* in the Piggly Wiggly parking lot. But despite all this, I climbed into my car, crawled into the front seat, and began the drive to see Mom, go to church, cleanse myself of her imagined and presumably accurate sins, and get a home-cooked meal. The last part was probably the real reason I hopped in the car.

It was only an hour and a half drive, so I figured I'd be okay in the Chevette. As usual, I was wrong. It was one of those unbelievably hot and muggy days in Tennessee. I was sweating. Not a southern girl's *glow*. I was *sweatin'!* Every time I hit a pothole, the hatchback would shut, which was a disaster because keeping the hatchback open provided the only ventilation I had. With each mile, I got madder and madder. I was working two jobs to try and stay in school, I missed my sisters, it was 95 degrees, I was drenched, and the hatchback was now shut tight. I was beyond hot, and I was so tired that I worried I might fall asleep at the wheel. And I didn't want to die in the Chevette because that would be too humiliating. I could see the headline: "SWEAT-SOAKED PREACHER'S DAUGHTER FRIES TO DEATH IN CHEVETTE—FOUND CLUTCHING A HALF-BAKED POTATO."

But ol' Chonda had an idea to get me through this ordeal.

I told the Lord, "You're not going to get me. I'll sing a song to stay awake. I'll sing every cool song on the radio." Three Dog Night. Fifth Dimension. Michael Jackson before his surgeries.

I figured with any luck I'd hear a song by my cornbread-and-beans friend Tanya Tucker and distract myself. So I reached over to turn the radio on, and the knob broke. That was it! I wanted to throw the knob out the window, but I couldn't do that because I couldn't roll the window down. My life was officially in the pits. I'd had it with the Lord. I thought if He wasn't going to help me, I'd just handle it myself. I decided to sing to myself for an hour and a half without the radio—in alphabetical order.

*A . . . A . . . A . . .* I was stumped. What Three Dog Night song begins with A? Every song I could think of was a church song!

A . . . Amazing Grace
Blessed Assurance, Jesus Is Mine
Come and Dine (the Master Calleth)
Deep and Wide, Deep and Wide
Every Day with Jesus Is Sweeter Than the Day Before
Feeling at Home in the Presence of Jesus
God Is So Good
How Great Thou Art
Into My Heart
Jesus Loves Me This I Know, for the Bible Tells Me So

(By the way, for those reading this, it's even better on the audiobook version.)

Kumbaya, My Lord, Kumbaya
Love Lifted Me
My Jesus, I Love You
No One Ever Cared for Me
Oh, How I Love Jesus
People Need the Lord
There Is a Quiet Place
Rolled Away
Standing on the Promises
Trust and Obey for There's No Other Way
Undeserving of Your Love
Victory in Jesus

Then came W . . . and this song:

What a friend we have in Jesus,
All our sins and griefs to bear!
What a privilege to carry
Everything to God in prayer!
Oh, what peace we often forfeit,
Oh, what needless pain we bear,
All because we do not carry
Everything to God in prayer!

Have we trials and temptations?
Is there trouble anywhere?
We should never be discouraged,
Take it to the Lord in prayer.
Can we find a friend so faithful,
Who will all our sorrows share?
Jesus knows our every weakness,
Take it to the Lord in prayer.[1]

A tear rolled down my cheek, and soon my eyes were so blurry I had to pull off the road. The line "all our sins and griefs to bear" struck me as so profound, I began to sob. I had always known Jesus bore my sins, and I carried them to Him often, but it hadn't occurred to me that He would carry my grief. I had been trying to carry all that weight on my own. I didn't think God wanted to hear about my grief. The realization of His fathomless love was overwhelming in that moment.

It's one thing to know Jesus as your Savior who died for your sins and be grateful for that, but when you get to a level where you know Him as a friend, it's a game changer because it becomes intimate. God is no longer the big man up there waiting to pound you because your

1 "What a Friend We Have in Jesus," lyrics by Joseph M. Scriven, 1865, public domain.

skirt isn't long enough. And He's not the God who created so much that you are only a small detail in the universe. That song reminded me that He brings himself down to a personal level with us to allow us to call Him friend, and a true friend is someone you can unload your burdens on. I believe the Holy Spirit used that old hymn to remind me of truths I had heard as a little child, and I think that's what makes Christian music powerful. It hits you on a deep level on the days you need it.

Every time I hear or sing that song, whether in 1980 or today, I break into tears. That day was no different. And I am so glad the Holy Spirit showed up in my Chevette right then, because the Lord knows I would never have thought of a song that began with the letter X. I'd still be circling Nashville.

Wait. I just thought of it. Xanadu!

## CHAPTER 5

# MARRIAGE AND MOTHERHOOD

Just because I had a personal revival in my Chevette didn't mean I became a squeaky-clean and ultra-proper Christian girl. I still had a lot of growing up and healing to do, so—spoiler alert—there will be some confessions in this chapter. Try not to judge.

Around this time, David was attending Middle Tennessee State University, and I was in college at Austin Peay about ninety minutes away. We wrote letters to each other because there were no cellphones back then. For readers younger than twenty years old, a letter is what happens when you take a pen and paper and write your thoughts down after careful consideration of what you want to say, as opposed to banging out a text while driving that is full of misspellings that cause a huge fight because instead of saying "I love you," you accidentally typed "I loathe you."

But somewhere along the way, the letters back and forth between David and me got a little more personal. Slowly we became more romantic, and by the time I was twenty-one, we were seeing each other every weekend.

The real mystery was why it took so long. *Everyone* loved David. My mother loved David. My brother loved David. All long before I did. Looking back, the demise of most of my boyfriends started when my family began to like them more than I did. And the more my family disapproved, the longer I would keep the guy around!

But not David. He outlasted everyone. I couldn't help but love him. He was good-looking, funny, and steady. We called it *rock steady* back then. David was charmingly predictable. Never overly emotional. (Okay, he may have gotten excited at Vanderbilt basketball games or Atlanta Braves baseball games, and I wish he could see Vanderbilt baseball today. Go Commodores!)

Even after David and I started getting serious, we occasionally dated other people. I mean, if you buy the first car you drive, you could end up with a Chevette or worse—like a Datsun your dad steals . . . did I mention that? On weekends when I was home in Nashville, we would visit and tease each other about our ridiculous dating choices. And as you know, we eventually married each other.

But first a confession: the life skills I learned by the time I was twenty-one involved how to make fried chicken, fried mashed potato patties, and a fervent belief in the fact that bacon grease is a must in every kitchen. I could thread a needle and sew a new dress. But I knew nothing about sex, drugs, or rock and roll. So, I learned about much of that on my own. Not the drugs part, or the rock and roll part, which was on the radio. But the other one . . .

I was away at school and lonely. I was already well acquainted with grief, but I knew nothing about my raging hormones. So, when a very handsome guy would flirt with me, well, almost all my boundaries were tossed out of the window. The theater department at Austin Peay was not filled with church kids like Trevecca had been. Many of the boys were gay, and the ones who were not took "Casanova" to a whole new level. At every cast party or set-building gathering, the girls would giggle and talk about their sexual encounters and try to one-up each other with who had gone the furthest with the greatest number of boys. Me? I was almost twenty-two and had no experience with sex. Oh, once at Trevecca the "big man" on campus took me parking. He tried to teach me about oral sex by *coercion*. He must have thought that was romance! I just thought he was weird.

By the way, guys, that *never* works. Flowers, dinner, and compliments maybe, but pressure on the back of the neck? Nope! I think I actually said to him, "You want me to do *what*? Are you crazy? That's just gross." I know—harsh and graphic, but that was my mindset at the time.

Back to my confession. I met an older guy while working a part-time job. Don't worry, it wasn't like he was seventy and I was twenty-one. It was Tennessee, not Hollywood. I was a hotel desk clerk in the evenings because the hours were flexible with my theater schedule. The hotel staff were alumni of most of the local colleges in the area, and one man was both newly divorced and attractive. One evening he invited me to his apartment for a glass of wine. His invitation was different. It sounded so adult and sophisticated to me. I rationalized that it was okay because wine is in the Bible.

I'd had very little contact with alcohol of any kind before that, except for at my first theater party at Austin Peay where a couple of friends invited me to try a shot of tequila. I was clueless but curious, so I agreed to taste it. "First, lick your hand" (a little gross if you ask me!), "then sprinkle salt on your hand," they said. "Then lick the salt off, toss back the tiny 'communion cup' of tequila, then squeeze lemon juice into your mouth real quick." I followed their instructions carefully and immediately coughed and blurted out, "Ugh! This tastes like alcohol!" The room erupted in laughter. Apparently, tequila wards off any germs you might absorb from your dirty hands. Note to all: 1. Tequila *is* alcohol. 2. Tequila shots are way too much trouble!

My mother warned me about my coworker in advance, even though she had never met him. "Divorced men are going to want more of you than men who have never been married," which is 100 percent not true. All men are pretty much the same. But I digress. I disregarded my mom's warning, went home with him, and drank my very first glass of wine. And to be honest, I wanted to have sex. I was curious to know what the fuss around it was all about. Without getting too graphic again, I'll just say it was terrible, it was painful, and it was quick.

It wasn't intimate or romantic, and I felt terrible right afterward. I felt even worse when I found out he had a big bet with other guys at work about who would be "the one" to nail me. And the lesson I learned was that all the preaching in the world is not going to slow down a lonely, hormonal twenty-one-year-old. The only remedy for that is sharing an apartment with your mom in a senior center that smells like Vicks.

I felt even worse the next day as shame and embarrassment crept in. I had been taught to wait for marriage, and I hadn't. Although David and I didn't have an exclusive agreement, I felt I had betrayed him. And Mom, a.k.a. Sherlock Holmes, was hot on the trail of the criminal, even though she was miles away visiting Mike in Ohio. I called her and said, "Mother, something terrible has happened," and somewhere between the words *terrible* and *happened*, she knew exactly what it was. Mom would always ground me and punish me for small things, but when she thought I was in a place of great remorse, she was wonderful. "Honey," she said, "Jesus loves you just as much today as He did yesterday, and He can wash your sins away and make you a clean person before God again . . . By the way, did he have any protection?"

Being from Ashland City, Tennessee, I thought she was asking if he had a gun. When I said I didn't see a pistol, she said, "No, honey, the other kind of protection."

I replied, "It was dark, and I couldn't see, but I think he had something on."

"That's a condom, honey," she said.

While I was on the phone with her, David walked in, sat down next to me, and wrapped his arm around me. I spilled my guts to Mom as he patted my back and listened until I hung up the phone. Then I turned to him with tears leaking from my eyes and asked, "Do you think I'm terrible?"

"No," he replied. "Just give me his name so I can go kick his butt."

That was a pivotal moment in our relationship. David went from being a fun friend and a sometimes-boyfriend to a treasured confidant. There I was, confessing my ugliest sin to a guy, crying on his shoulder, and his response was kind and accepting. He handled something private with tenderness and grace when he could have called me a sleaze, and that tipped the scale toward a deeper intimacy. I often wish I had recognized David as my one and only earlier, but I guess I was too naïve to see it just then.

In the following months, I met another guy at Austin Peay. And maybe another. I don't know, math was never my strong suit. Trial and error. Mainly error. Probably doing exactly what the Johnny Lee country song says: "Looking for love in all the wrong places." At least at the next cast party or sorority gathering, I finally had my own notes to share. They say when a man tells you how many women he's been with, you divide by two, and with women you multiply by two. But in those sharing moments with the other girls, I realized I was doing some major comparisons. I would tell my friends I loved Pat, but he didn't have David's sense of humor; if he did, he'd be perfect. And when I was dating Danny, who was really talented, he didn't have David's looks. I thought if Pat were funny, I'd marry him, and if Danny were better looking, I'd marry him. Then it dawned on me—the only guy as funny and good-looking and talented as David... was David. So, I crawled through the hatchback into my Chevette, turned the radio knob which fell off again, shifted the potato into first gear, and drove right to David's dorm at college.

I walked into his room and said, "David, I made my decision. You're the one. Let's start dating seriously and get married."

I stood there with open arms and trembling lips, waiting for him to rush over and kiss me. This was going to be a rom-com movie ending; it was the moment every young girl who loved Cinderella and Snow White was waiting for. Okay, at that point I wasn't Snow White; to reference Mae West, I had drifted. But this was my moment. And instead of rushing over to plant a kiss on my lips, David stood there and said, "I've got to go. I have a date tonight."

What? I was rejected? That never happens. I was furious. How dare he see other women when I had been true and faithful and completely done seeing other men for at least five whole minutes. But David was the smartest. The more he played "hard to get," the more I was completely smitten. After all the trials and tribulations I had put him through, he was going to make me work for it. The nerve of him. But give me a challenge and I *will* overcome it! It took about three days! (Okay, he didn't play *that* hard to get.) From then on, we were a couple. When we decided to "get serious," we did serious very well. We were never happier. We began to piece together not just two very dysfunctional and broken lives, we pieced together our *one* life.

David had found a job as a maintenance man for a hotel on the edge of town, and I decided to apply for the desk clerk job there. This worked out perfectly as the hotel manager gave us two adjoining rooms to make a small apartment—it would be our first home together after the wedding. We spent months painting and putting in a small kitchenette. We found a couch sitting next to a dumpster, and I took the old sheets that the hotel was throwing away, then spent days boiling them in fabric dye to make curtains, bedspreads, and tablecloths. We were excited, madly in love, and very physically attracted to one another.

So, "making out" on our new dumpster couch became more and more tempting, and one night after painting what would soon be our new bathroom, I discovered that passion with David was more than special. I'd never imagined intimacy could be so tender. I thought, "So *this* is what God intended. A true expression of love. Real love. Committed love."

I was twenty-three when we got married. The prior Christmas, David gave me a used sewing machine, which he probably found during another dumpster dive. But it worked and I loved to sew. I made my own wedding dress. The fabric was about $100, which was donated, thanks to Mom. That much money was hard for her to gather up, but somehow, she did it. I went to the fabric store and bought the white satin and beautiful lace, and for the next three months, I stitched during every spare minute.

Finally, we had a place to live, I had my dress, and we were all set for the ceremony. The night before my wedding, my mom pulled me aside for "the talk." Since she knew about the young man and the wine, it was a little late for the birds and the bees, but she had to have her say. She said, "Chonda, let's have a talk about s-e-x." I guess she wanted me to know about married sex, which apparently is different from single sex.

She handed me a brochure and told me to read it and ask her any questions. The brochure was about how to make a roast on Sunday night because men want a roast at least once a week. From what I hear, some men like a rump roast. Get your mind out of the gutter; it was a food joke, not a sex joke. But how is this a metaphor? How will this help a young woman if you say sex is like a roast? That could be so confusing. Does foreplay involve salt and pepper and a meat tenderizer? And what if you marry a vegan?

Twenty-four hours later, I was a bride prepared to give David a nice brisket. We had a very romantic honeymoon. As we left the farmhouse porch where we said our vows, David looked me in the eyes, took me by the hand, and said, "I'm going to show you the world." I practically swooned thinking, *This is great, he's going to take me to Geneva and Paris and Rome.* Instead, he took me to Disney's Epcot theme park. For one day. That's all we could afford, so we saw Switzerland and France in twenty minutes because we only had enough money to see the world in one day!

When we came back from our romantic "world tour," we moved into our little hotel apartment at the Econo Lodge just off the interstate in Nashville. It was exactly what you would expect—paper-thin walls, a broken air-conditioning unit, and a mouthy desk clerk. Thankfully, David was an amazing maintenance man. After he took wiring classes, he could fix anything. I kept my job as desk clerk in the winter and worked at Opryland in the summer. More on that later.

And then, the unimaginable happened. Although we had a gun for protection, I got pregnant. How did this happen? My fault. Since I knew we would be having roasts a lot more often once we were married, I went and got birth control pills about two days before our wedding. Nobody told me it didn't work overnight, so I got pregnant probably between "Switzerland" and "France" at Epcot! We went to the beach to get a little sun, and I got a little daughter instead. Say that last sentence out loud for the laugh.

I was sick the entire pregnancy. I threw up everything. Remember Linda Blair with the pea soup in *The Exorcist*? That was me the minute food touched my lips. Finally, someone suggested saffron rice and that worked. I ate it three times a day.

I managed to work through the summer at Opryland—although they don't serve saffron rice there—but at four months pregnant, I started having horrible pains in my abdomen. I panicked, thinking I was in labor. I prayed to God to save my baby until the pain grew so great that I had to go to the hospital.

The contractions were coming fast and furious, and I was only four and a half months pregnant. They ran an ultrasound and about an hour later the doctor came in with a gastroenterologist. And they announced that I had a medical condition a lot of people have suspected about me for years. The doctor looked me in the eye, took my hand, and said, "You're full of crap."

Seriously, I was so constipated. I wasn't in labor, and the large mass just below my uterus was not a tumor. It was so full of saffron rice that I was experiencing what in precise medical terms doctors called "the full Elvis."

They asked me the last time I had a bowel movement, and I couldn't remember. Although I did say I hadn't bought any toilet paper since Memorial Day. Of course, they couldn't give me any medicine because of the baby, so they had to give me an enema. Correction, they had to give me fourteen enemas to get all the crap out of me. It was the first time in Tennessee history that a nurse had to administer a basic medical procedure wearing a hazmat suit.

Every day for the rest of my pregnancy, I had to start the morning with that bag of water. Before breakfast. And my husband had to help. We were newlyweds, so talk about humiliating, and trust me, the last thing a man wants after giving someone an enema in the morning is to enjoy a roast later that night. But David was amazing; part saint, part nurse, part handyman. He put a nail in the wall and would hang the enema bag there, run the tube up under a sheet, then give me a kiss and say, "There you go, hon" before heading off to work. As he was leaving, I was going . . . and going . . . and going. How lovely.

Instead of romantically remembering our wedding vows, it was more like remembering my wedding bowels.

That last line looks stupid in print but is hilarious to say out loud on stage.

Meanwhile, I was losing more weight than a supermodel. I weighed about 100 pounds on our honeymoon, and I was down to 86 pounds when our daughter finally came. I started to cry on the way to the hospital. "What's the matter?" David asked.

"Tomorrow we will be married nine months, and I know my mother will do the math." We had our doctor, two lawyers, and three friends sign affidavits that I delivered our daughter, Chera, six weeks early so my mother would stop wringing her hands. But the truth is, it wouldn't have mattered to Mom, because when we put that tiny new granddaughter in her hands, she never mentioned it again.

## CHAPTER 6

# A STAR IS BORN, ALMOST

People often ask how I ended up on the stage of the world-famous Grand Ole Opry. It certainly didn't happen overnight. My entry into professional show business came with my first job at Opryland USA just before David and I got married. Nashville was bursting with country music fans in the early 1980s, so Gaylord Entertainment built an amazing theme park wrapped around the newly built Grand Ole Opry House in the early '70s. Millions visited the theme park, and it was a great place for young wannabe performers and dancers to hone their craft without a two-drink minimum! The baby steps I took in the summer of 1982 were in many ways the first steps on my amazing forty-year show business journey.

I knew very little about country music. Or any secular music for that matter. Remember, my dad did not allow us to listen to *worldly* music. And when I secretly did, it wasn't country; I listened to Top 40—Earth, Wind & Fire; Jimmy Buffet; Three Dog Night. But regardless of my lack of country music roots, I loved music, plus I had the acting bug. Whether in high school or colleges—that's right, colleges plural. Remember, I had a checkered academic career—I was in every play and was always in community theater. It started when I was little and played Mayor Shinn's younger daughter in *The Music Man* at the community theater in Myrtle Beach. By the time I was in college, I was Zaneeta Shinn, the teenage daughter.

Funny flashback, the very conservative Christian college I went to censored *The Music Man*. As a theater major, I remember going to the student director. "Really? You're taking out 'Shipoopi'?" Without the dance number in the library with Harold Hill, you mess up the storyline and why the kids in River City need more to do. But they were not going to allow a song that sounded like "poopy." Or included dancing. They were never sure at that school if dancing led to sex or sex led to dancing. Either way, they were against it.

When I left that very meek and mild conservative theater, I dove headfirst into a very liberal university theater at Austin Peay where my $300 acting scholarship garnered me a job in the costume department.

And the first play they let me be involved in was a Greek comedy called *Lysistrata*. In case you don't know the plot, *Lysistrata* is a comedy written by Aristophanes about...uh...let's just say a woman on a mission to end the war by convincing all the women to deny all the men sex. In other words, no roasts.

My first task in that liberal theater was to stitch pink penises into men's underwear to show just how much the men were in need of women. The other girls would tease "the little Christian girl" as I sewed while wiping the blushing sweat off my forehead. I was really flustered when they told me one of the penises was Jewish. Later when I saw the statue of the David, I understood. I found it hard to sew and keep my eyes closed without pricking my fingers. I was convinced my front row seat in the handbasket to hell was sealed at last. Eventually, I escaped the costume department and got to act and sing, and soon

I was trying to bridge the gap between the drama department and the music department.

Then my big break came. One of my professors, Dr. Mabry, introduced me to Joe Jerles, a director at Opryland. Years before *American Idol* and *The Voice*, Opryland decided to hold auditions for college students around the country to see who could work there. We had about eight seconds to sing part of a song to wow a panel of music directors and choreographers. I was on my way, and I was going to be a superstar. Bradley Cooper discovered Lady Gaga in *A Star Is Born*, and Joe Jerles was going to make me a star. So, I prepared, went to an audition...and they turned me down. I didn't even get a callback.

Are you ready? They said I was too skinny! I was skinny-shamed! Well, for the last thirty-eight years, I have made sure at every mealtime that no one could ever say that again. Other actresses had to purge; I had to gorge.

Thankfully, they didn't dismiss me out of hand; they said to come back the next year. So, while I was sewing my wedding dress and planning my life with David, I got ready, and I went back after my honeymoon. After I finished singing an entire song, the general manager, Bob Whitaker, stood from the panel and turned to the small audience of performers, writers, and musicians. "Young people, pay attention," he said. "That is how you sell a song. A missed note here and there, it doesn't matter. She sang like she meant every word."

To this day Joe Jerles says, "I knew it when she walked in. I knew she had that elusive 'it factor.'" Did he mean charisma? Chemistry? The extra ten pounds? If they could bottle "it," people would sell their soul for it. I always wonder where I got "it." Maybe it was all those years of singing in church; or maybe it was all those miles of singing in my Chevette, but whatever it was, it paid off.

The powers that be figured if I could sing, I could learn to dance, so I began working at Opryland as a singer/dancer. Thirty-seven years later, I still run into Bob Whitaker, his wife Jean (who was the park's choreographer), and Joe Jerles. And thirty-seven years later, we still laugh at the fact that I never did learn how to dance. No matter how hard I tried. Thank goodness there was a part in the show they put me in that would exclude me from the big dance ensemble. It was a comedy sketch, and Joe Jerles handed me two pages of jokes to memorize—funny country stories of Minnie Pearl and her life in Grinders Switch, Tennessee.

People liked it! And for the next six years, I impersonated Minnie Pearl at the theme park as well as at special events around Nashville, and even area churches looking for clean entertainment.

Okay, let's take a break from talking about me (Alert the media, Chonda is going to talk about someone other than herself!) and let me tell you about one of my heroes, the real Minnie Pearl. I have a lot of comedy heroes—like Carol Burnett and Lucille Ball—but Minnie was both a comedian and a personal hero. Like Carol Burnett, her show always seemed clean, well-rounded, and hilarious. Same with Ellen DeGeneres and Roseanne Barr's early stand-up performances on TV.

Minnie's real name was Sarah Ophelia Colley Cannon, and she was a country comedian who performed at the Grand Ole Opry for half a century. All of America knew her from her appearances on *Match Game* and *Hollywood Squares*. She dressed funny, she talked funny, and most important, she *was* funny. In her frilly dress and her hat with a price tag still attached, she greeted everyone with "Howww-DEEEEE! I'm just so proud to be here!" My job was to go on stage as Minnie and do my impersonation as if I were from Grinder's Switch, Tennessee.

I got to meet the real Minnie several times. Once was when I was three months pregnant and had been asked to do my Minnie impersonation at a corporate event in Nashville. When I went backstage to get ready to go on, the first person I saw was Sarah Cannon, the real Minnie, in her street clothes. My first thought was that there had been a mix-up and she was supposed to perform. I started to apologize, and she interrupted. "Honey, this is your night. I just wanted to see what Minnie Pearl looked like pregnant."

I felt sad at first, thinking she was lamenting the fact that she had never had kids. It wasn't until later that I realized she just wanted to make sure I wasn't showing. She had an image and a brand and the last thing she wanted people to think was that a single gal like Minnie had gotten knocked up in Grinder's Switch.

Another time, I got to share a dressing room with her. Think about it. That's like a young singer getting to share a dressing room with Frank Sinatra. I asked questions about the early years of country music. She had a plethora of wild stories about Patsy Cline and her foul mouth, and after each one, Minnie would punctuate it with, "Bless her heart."

As fun as that was, Minnie gave me more than a start to my career and some wild Patsy Cline stories. She gave me advice that I took to heart then and still follow during every performance. One day, she gathered a few of us together and told us a story. Her life dream was to be a Broadway star. One night as she was working at the Ryman—the original stage of the Grand Ole Opry—there were only five or six people in the audience, just a few people sitting in the hot, old-fashioned auditorium which had no air conditioning. A little upset there was no crowd, she turned her back on the audience, spun the microphone around, and faced the band, telling her funny stories to the musicians and the radio audience listening. She paid very little attention to the men sitting on the front row. After the show, one of the men approached her and said they were from New York. They had heard so much about her that they had come to Nashville to see if she would be right for a major part in

*Annie Get Your Gun.* He said he was sorry, but they were no longer interested because she had shown a lack of professionalism. She had no idea it was an audition, and she had blown it. She then told each of us who were listening wide-eyed to her story to treat every show as if it's the biggest in your life and give 100 percent to the audience, whether you're in front of five people or five thousand. I have never forgotten her words.

Entertaining in a theme park is probably not filled with the perils of life in the fast lane like those of real showbiz. There are no paparazzi, although we had regular fans like my mom who rarely missed a day. Working at Opryland, I didn't get to rub elbows with real artists often, but I did get to be in the company of some young performers who later became real artists. Tim Rushlow and a small band of rockers did the '50s show at the park and went on to become the group Little Texas. Then there were Marty Roe and Dan Truman, who became founding members in the group Diamond Rio. Steven Curtis Chapman went on to become, well, Steven Curtis Chapman.

Jerry Salley and I performed in the same show for years. He is a bluegrass artist and well-known songwriter in Nashville. We were both in a very select, small, and elite group at Opryland—married performers—which comes with a different set of circumstances than the single, party-going young 'uns. Jerry and I both had small children. His wife, Emily, and I became fast friends, and as married couples, we hung out with them a lot during the summer. With our one day off each week, we cooked out, and David and Emily took turns pushing baby buggies around the park on the other six days until Jerry and I were off the stage.

I loved watching David and Chera while I was singing. I'd be belting out a verse of "Stand by Your Man" while David and Chera twirled on the teacups, my baby girl squealing with delight. One time, as the show started, I saw David walk by, pushing Chera in the stroller. They were headed to the carnival games, no kiddie rides that day. David had decided he was going to teach Chera the art of winning. They disappeared out of sight, and I could only imagine David tossing rings around Coca-Cola bottles or shooting the bullseye with the water gun. Soon they came back, this time with Chera pushing the stroller, and in it sat a giant bear bigger than David. David walked along behind her with the silliest grin on his face.

As I finished the last number and headed backstage to meet them, the cast crowded around David, cracking up at his story as he told them what had happened. He had started with ten dollars to teach her how to win. He was down to his last dollar, and nothing was working. It was that game where you get three rings for a dollar, and you can toss them onto the standing Coke bottles to win a prize. Every few minutes, Chera would tug on David's arm and ask for a turn. "In just a minute, honey. Daddy's gonna win something big for you."

Another dollar, three more tosses. Still nothing. Finally, Chera pulled at his shirt tail and pleaded, "Daddy, can I throw them this time?" Mumbling to himself how these things must be rigged, he handed her the three metal rings. She was so tiny that the man at the carnival game gave her a stool to stand on. Toss one, two, and three. Chera flicked her little wrist about that fast, and each ring landed with a *ping, ping, ping* perfectly around the tops of the bottles. Without hesitation, she dusted her hands and said, "There you go, Daddy. We won. Now can we go ride rides?"

During my time at Opryland, David and I did some growing up, as did our possessions. Our tiny house led to another one slightly bigger. The Chevette went to Chevy heaven after we replaced it with a minivan. And David started a quest to explore his creative side. Even while working at his maintenance job, he would find time to write—mainly short stories for *Ellery Queen's Mystery Magazine* and *Alfred Hitchcock's Mystery Magazine*. He *loved* to write. But even with all his talent, he couldn't seem to break out as an author. For every little gig I would get singing or impersonating Minnie Pearl, he got another letter in a growing stack of rejections.

When one half of a couple is in show business and the other half isn't, there can be problems. Me having a show business career and David's working as a maintenance man was in some ways at the heart of the challenges we eventually had. Chris Rock has a great segment in his special (*Tamborine*) where he says every relationship is like a band: someone has to be the lead singer, and someone has to play the tambourine. And a lot of times the person playing the tambourine is not going to be happy. I always tried to include David in my work because he was creative, but it's a challenge when one person is the lead and the other doesn't even like the tambourine. There is resentment and there are temptations; there is a need to punish and a desire to have someone validate that you are more than a tambourine player. More on that later.

I met some performers who made a long career out of being a park performer. But I wanted more. And David and I wanted more; we wanted another baby. I knew the summer heat and physical exertion would not be conducive to cooking up more roasts. So, after six years, I decided to leave Opryland. It was time to move on, and I walked away figuring I would never return.

So, what next? I decided to take the first step toward my new dream of being a superstar singer, and I had heard the road to winning that Grammy in Nashville was to work as a song plugger and start singing demos. Little did I know back then that one day I would make it to the greatest stage of all—the Grand Ole Opry.

## CHAPTER 7

# TAKING ON MUSIC ROW

My friend from Opryland, Jerry Salley, was writing songs on the world-famous Music Row, and he told me one of his publishers was looking for a secretary. I took the job.

Okay, another confession, although this one is not as personal as the last half dozen: I was not a secretary.

Although I would have been a good one, other than the fact I couldn't type, hated to file, and wasn't the best speler. I mean spealer. Wait (imagine the sound of Chonda sounding out each letter) . . . speller!

I kept Wite-Out in business for the first three weeks on the job. On the plus side, my phone skills were excellent, and I could make coffee better than most. Now, there are a lot of biographies of stars from the late '80s and early '90s that talk about how these women were secretaries and then—poof!—one day they were humming a song at their desk, the record executive heard them, they sang a few notes out loud, signed $20 million-dollar record deals, and became famous singers! That did not happen to yours truly . . . and I could sing!

In the late '70s and early '80s, the old saying, "sleeping your way to the top" wasn't just a rumor—I think for some women in the music business, it was a business plan. Hopefully you have figured out that I did not sleep my way to the top of anything. I didn't even sleep my way to the middle. By this time in my life with David, I was completely smitten with love and commitment. Our sex life was a beautiful extension of our undying love for one another. The thought of a man other than David touching my body sickened me. So, when I got my job on Music Row with a very public and successful publisher, each one of his sexual innuendos, his trying to press me up against the copy machine, the daily pats on the butt, were disgusting. Yes, all of that happened. To me and every woman in the office. No names—he knows who he is. In fact, let all the music executives back then who are the reason we have #MeToo think I just might reveal their names and ruin their squeaky-clean images. Maybe they will come to my next live performance to see if I name them! Nah, most of them are dead!

These DOM (dirty old men, and not all were old) operated with the idea that a tryst with them here and there—you scratch my back (or front), I'll scratch yours—would garner you a record deal. And sadly, far too often, it was true. I know of several country music superstars who deep down regret that their climb to the top had less to do with their vocal talents and more with their horizontal talents. They sold bits and pieces of themselves for a chance at the brass ring.

The music business is full of these narcissistic men and a few opportunistic women; then again, so is every business from politics to preaching. It seems like every day we read another story about a movie producer or a television executive who wants a private meeting in a hotel room to discuss your career and by the way, it's "open bathrobe Friday." They use their positions of power to try and get you to do what you know is wrong. I never gave in to that man, but I still had to put up with the groping and grabbing.

It usually started when he would go out to lunch and have a couple of drinks. Around 2:30 in the afternoon, he would wander back into the office, call me in for a meeting, and the next thing you'd know, there'd be a hand reaching where the sun don't shine. I would go home so upset. One solution was for me to ask David to please stop by my office more often. He began to meet me at the office for lunch or bring me dinner if I had to work late. But honestly, it didn't matter how many times these men saw you with your husband—they saw all of us as Dolly Parton in *9 to 5*.

But David and I needed the money, and I had to work to keep it coming in, so I just dealt with it. I didn't dare slap my boss because then he would fire me. And those are the moments that haunted me the most—when I didn't stand up for myself, when I wasn't strong, when I didn't just walk away. Instead, I would go home and complain to David. "I don't trust my boss." "That man is a jerk." "This one is cheating on his wife."

David would say, "Well keep your guard up, hon. We need the money." Then he'd go back to writing.

In retrospect, I realize now that this big-time music executive reminded me of a man I had been spending most of my life avoiding—my dad. They were one and the same—men of power who left behind them a trail of exploited women. I'm sure with my dad, many of these women must have been thinking, "This man is so God-like, he can get me into heaven." For some women, heaven is heaven; for others, heaven is a record deal.

Finally, I found a way out. My lifeline was Judy Harris, a female record executive during a time when they were few and far between. Kind of like now. Change that, Nashville! I was drawn to strong women like Judy in the business. They were determined and focused, and they had the brass ovaries to push back and slap hands. They weren't in the "good ole boys" club, and they couldn't care less. In my first conversation with Judy, I told her I was working for John Schmoo (you know that's not his real name). She shook her head as if to say, "You poor thing!" As we talked, she gave me incredible advice in just two words. "Get out!" Ha! Well, it was couched in a long conversation about mustering strength and determining your worth, but it boiled down to "Get out!"

We had a great connection; she was Sarah Cannon's niece. Yes, the real Minnie Pearl had a niece. Judy hired me on the spot, and I started the next Monday working at Harris Richardson Music Group. The good news—there was zero harassment there. The bad news—I still had to work the party circuit with the same old men who were still enjoying their same old behavior. But this time, I had some defense mechanisms at my disposal, thanks to Judy Harris, who gave me advice on ways to cut them off and how to cleverly stay busy when they approached and keep my professional distance.

One of my jobs for Judy was to listen to cassettes and type up the lyrics. I would prepare the lyric sheet, fill out the copyright information, track down any other information for the songwriters I might need, and put it all on Judy's desk by day's end. And one of those days was life-changing. I had put in the cassette and started typing the words to a song called "The Saving Kind."

My life was filled with darkness
And no matter where I turned
There was no light
And in my desperation
And loneliness I cried out in the night

And I know there is a God
Lord, I know you're out there somewhere
Please come tonight
As I fell to my knees
I felt the power of a love
I call the saving kind

The brightest light I've ever seen was shining
The warmest breeze was flowing through my life
The greatest peace I've ever known has filled me
Ever since I felt the power of the love
I call the saving kind

When life gets you down
And no matter who you're with, you're still alone
And you know there must be more to life
Than feeling like you're far away from home
And you've almost given up
On ever finding everlasting peace of mind
Well believe me when I tell you
That the love you're needing now's the saving kind

The brightest light I've ever seen was shining
The warmest breeze was flowing through my life
The greatest peace I've ever known has filled me
Ever since I felt the power of the love
I call the saving kind
Jesus is the reason for the love
We call the saving kind[1]

---

1 "The Saving Kind," Brian Free, *Call of the Cross*, Capitol CMG, 2001.

Something happened with each line I typed. It was mysterious. Divine. A tear dropped from my eyes onto the keyboard, and soon it was a blubberfest, and I couldn't stop. It was like the meaning and power of the words and the simple melody sank deep into my heart. The song was so tender about the saving love of God and the power of the Holy Spirit. It was also intense but in a soft, wooing way that drew me in. It was just what I needed to seal a resolve, water a seed. Whatever that is that comes when you know that you know that you know, "Sunday morning Christian just doesn't work for me anymore." The truth is, David and I had become "sleep-in-Sunday Christians," and deep down, I was hungry for more. A deeper walk and true relationship. A love that is the saving kind.

With each line I typed, I cried harder and harder until it became too much. I ran into the bathroom and threw up. It was like I was purging out the memories of all the ungodly circumstances I had been surrounded by—the drunken men, the sexist remarks, the grabbing hands. And even though it would be a few decades before I would come to grips with the pain hidden deep in my heart, in that moment in a bathroom on 17th Avenue, Music Row, in Nashville, Tennessee, my life changed forever. In perfect comedic fashion, I knelt before God's throne while kneeling at the throne.

After I cleaned myself up—and what a lovely sight I must have been—I walked into Judy's office and told her I needed to go home.

"Okay," she said, "when do you think you'll be back?"

"Miss Judy, I don't think I'll ever be back," I answered.

My dream to be the next Reba McEntire was over. I left the office and got in my car—thank God it wasn't the Chevette, and we know it wasn't my stolen Datsun because my dad still had it. I picked up my daughter at daycare and drove home. David met me on the porch and knew something was up. We sat down, and I broke the news that I was giving my life wholly to Jesus and had quit my job. I'll never forget his initial reaction, "That's really great, honey. But did Jesus tell you to quit your job?"

In my heart, I think Jesus did. I told David about the song and how I didn't feel strong enough to keep working in such a loose environment. I told him how I wanted to focus on one thing: raising our daughter, Chera, in a home that included Jesus. Then I announced that I believed Jesus would help us get through, which was putting a lot on Jesus's shoulders. He is very busy saving souls, so I'm guessing He doesn't always have time to chat with mortgage companies and bill collectors. I prayed He would make an exception for me.

As I began the new phase of my life as a stay-at-home mom, I decided to try to do everything 100 percent perfectly. Be a mom, a wife, hold yard sales—not necessarily dressed as Raggedy Ann—cook the meals, everything. And then a miracle happened. Maybe Jesus did look at my credit score, and maybe He said, "Hold on everybody. I'll get back to making the blind man see in a minute. This girl really needs help now."

Lo and behold, the church my mom was attending announced they needed a minister of music and a church secretary—or maybe Mom told them they needed one! Mom and Jesus always were a powerful combination. Either way, I got the job—for the exorbitant salary of fifty dollars per week. I played the piano and directed the choir, and David and I taught the teenagers in Sunday school class. It was a massive megachurch that had . . . wait for it . . . as many as eighty people in attendance on Easter Sunday!

One window closed and another opened. A very small window, but a window nevertheless. And for a woman used to crawling into a Chevette through the hatchback, it was big enough. Between what

David was making, my fifty-dollar weekly salary, and my occasional Minnie Pearl routine for different groups at $150 a pop, we felt prosperous. Okay, maybe not prosperous, but we were fine.

During that same season, I got a call from South Central Bell. They had a big corporate event in Dallas and wanted to set up their next convention in Nashville. They asked me to take the stage as Minnie Pearl so the audience would get the Nashville country connection. I was supposed to introduce the president of the company.

I did my Minnie Pearl routine, then got my cue to wrap up. I introduced the president and . . . silence. Twenty thousand people stared at me while I stared toward the backstage waiting for the company president to show up. Finally, after what seemed like fifteen minutes but was probably more like a minute, he walked on stage. Apparently, he was unaware that there is nothing more anticlimactic than a big introduction followed by nothing. We were losing the crowd's attention and patience every second. So, I took my Minnie Pearl hat off and pulled a piece of paper out of the top of it (my cheat sheet) and started to ad lib. But not as Minnie. For the first time on stage, I was just Chonda. As he walked toward me, I said, "Oh, there you are. I'm so glad you're here. There's a call here on my phone bill. I know I did not make this call. I figured you were the man to see." The crowd roared laughing.

As silly and simple as it seems—THAT was *the* breakthrough moment in my career. I didn't get free phone service. I didn't get a bit of a standing ovation. But what I got was sheer unadulterated instinct. I trusted my own comedic instincts in front of an audience, and they liked me. I was Sally Field with an accent. They liked me, they really liked me. That moment clicked and got me thinking maybe, just maybe, I could do comedy as myself.

Most comics take the same path. Class clown, open mic nights, build a routine, go to comedy clubs like the Laugh Factory, the Improv, the Comedy Cellar, Mr. Giggles in Omaha (I made the last one up), finally become an emcee, and become a regular. Then they go on the road three hundred nights a year and land a TV special, a sitcom, or a late-night show. Jay Leno, Chris Rock, Rodney Dangerfield—they all took those steps. Of course, Chonda had to take a different route. I never worked out an act in a comedy club. I was just looking to make a living for my family, and talking worked best. Besides, me in a comedy club working in a dark room with glasses full of *alcohol* clanging? My mother would have shown up and dragged me out of there.

Right after that Dallas event, my brother invited David and me to join him and his wife, Doris, at a church convention where he was preaching in Florida. What a deal! Free hotel room, the kids could swim, and we figured we could sing some of our old songs together. We didn't hesitate for a second before saying yes. Mike said, "Bring your Minnie Pearl dress; they have a family fun night on Friday, and you can do that thing you do." That thing I do? No one got it. That thing I did was bringing in $150, which was $115.43 after taxes.

I didn't want to miss out on the free stuff or time with Mike, so I packed my Minnie gear and off we went. The head of the convention seemed delighted that I had my Minnie Pearl outfit with me. "Take the whole show for yourself," he said. *Wait . . . me?* I had a grand total of about fifteen minutes worth of stories as Minnie from Grinders Switch. How was I going to entertain for an hour? Despite my trepidation, I took the stage armed with just my mouth. I boldly belted out a "Howdee!" and did my Minnie routine. After about fifteen minutes, I then started to talk about growing up as a preacher's kid who sat on the "Second Row, Piano Side" and everyone started laughing, including me.

In case you didn't grow up like I did, your natural question is, "What is second, row piano side?"

Besides being the routine that launched my career, here is the summary. And yes, there might be a quiz at the end of this chapter. In the churches I grew up in, there were strict rules that nobody challenged. Things have changed since the late 1960s and early '70s, but back then, there were three primary rules for church services:

Rule #1: Piano on one side of the pulpit, organ on the other.

Rule #2: If the preacher is married, his wife must play the piano.

Rule #3: The preacher's kids must attend church.

You could not miss church for any reason. You could be wearing a body cast, and they would wheel you in and stand you up against the wall. Oh, and one subset to that rule: Children had to be 100 percent quiet and perfect.

Well, Rule #3, Subset A didn't work with me, so Mom would make us kids sit second row, piano side. That way, the minute I acted up, she could come over and smack me. Forget Usain Bolt. The all-time record for fastest human being is held by my mother. She'd be playing the old hymn "Victory in Jesus." I would get restless between the second and third verse. Somehow, she would leap from the piano bench, lecture me, smack my hand, and be back at the piano without missing a note.

The Florida convention audience ate that story up, so I continued.

"One time my dad was preaching, and his pants were unzipped." (And if you didn't skip the first few chapters of this book, you know that was not an unusual condition for him.) "As he walked to one side of the pulpit, folks who could see his fly open began to snicker. He'd step behind the pulpit, and people would settle down and listen. He'd start ranting again and step to the other side. People would start snickering on that side. Finally, my brother went to the back of the church and held up a sign that said, 'Dad, zip it up!' Dad thought Mike was trying to tell him to shut up. He glanced at his watch and addressed the congregation, 'I know you want me to zip it up, but I'm not gonna do it.'"

By then I was having so much fun, the stories kept coming.

My siblings and I didn't just get in trouble in church; we got in trouble everywhere, especially at home. For example, traveling evangelists often stayed at our house, and there was one who arrived with his cat named Georgette. He was so proud of that cat that he knitted little sweaters for her and put bows in her hair. That was one strange guy. I mean, if you saw that on his Match.com profile, would you date him? He is a definite Tinder swipe-left. When he was there, my mother would try to keep us busy and occupied away from him so we would not A) interrupt his godly work or B) embarrass her.

Her solution was to have all us kids go in the backyard and get busy painting an old picnic table. This worked out for a while . . . until the moment the evangelist's cat walked by, which immediately caused all of us to discuss what the cat would look like as a skunk. But why have a philosophical debate when we could find out for sure? After all, she was a black cat and we had white paint. And with just a few strokes of Sherwin-Williams #7006 Extra White, we painted a long stripe down her back. When the cat started meowing, my mother came out to see what was wrong. When she saw what we had done, she started crying. The evangelist heard Mom crying and the cat making a racket, which caused him to rush out of the house yelling, "You kids are carnal sinners! Carnal!"

I wish I had a video of it; it would have gone viral. The cat was screaming, we were laughing, the evangelist was yelling, and Mom was pleading, "You kids get the paint off that cat right now!" So, we found a can of turpentine, dumped it in a bucket, then dunked that cat repeatedly in that bucket. The cat when crazy, and when the evangelist got ready to go ballistic a second time, I yelled at him,

"Your cat is carnal! Carnal sinner!" Of course, I had no idea what *carnal* meant. Looking back, I guess I was anticipating it had something to do with the cat and the evangelist's wild tantrum. The evangelist then screamed even louder, accusing us of making the cat possessed, and he fled, leaving behind Georgette the cat, its bows, and its special menu. We got to keep the cat—we had him stuffed and mounted. (The cat, not the evangelist.)

After my megahit Florida show—okay, maybe it wasn't as big a hit as I tell people today—I was asked to speak at the big international Church of the Nazarene General Assembly. It's an event that happens every four years, and this time it was being held in Indianapolis. Almost sixty thousand leaders, parishioners, and pastors would be gathering for a week of teaching, policymaking, and inspiration. For me, it was the equivalent of what a five-minute set on *The Tonight Show* could do for a club comic. All I know is I got invited and was on my way, literally and figuratively. My mother was ecstatic. I sometimes wonder if it was a little redemption for her for all the trauma she experienced around my father.

Knowing how big the opportunity was, knowing what it could do for me, I felt extremely self-assured and confident. Wait, that typed itself. I was terrified. Seriously, it was scary and not just because of the huge audience—it was nerve-racking because I had been taught to keep secrets my whole life, and now I was being asked to tell my story in front of tens of thousands of people.

But I realized this was more than an opportunity to bring home some diaper money. It was a chance to test the waters to see if the church was truly ready to hear my testimony. The Reverend Tim Stearman was in charge of putting together the lineup of speakers and singers for that particular portion of the convention. He blatantly told me that he wanted me to speak out, he wanted the truth, he wanted the audience to learn what many preachers' kids and families really go through. Whether they were ready for my story—that was another matter, but those were the marching orders.

There was something incredibly healing about being invited to speak that day. The members of my childhood church wanted to hear my story? Great! I wasn't going to reveal all, and the words that came from me were mild, but it was the beginning of healing between me and a church that I never thought cared for those injured and pushed aside by the secrets in the pulpit.

So, I did what I could, and I peeled back a few of the layers of the onion, but not all. That's what this book is for. Back then, I said what I could say and waited to see if the world fell apart. It didn't, but there were things I knew I wasn't ready to share.

Like the fact my pastor father's abuse was sexual in nature.

Like the fact that when my mother ran for help, the church shut us down.

Like the fact my big sister endured a lot of pain before she died.

I'll never forget the last time Charlotta sang at the Wednesday night service at church. She sang, "Whatever It Takes," stopped in the middle of the song, stood up from the piano, moved the microphone, then walked to the altar and sobbed. Three days later, she was dead.

I found my sister's diary and read it after she died. In doing so, I learned so much about her, things I didn't know, things I wish she could have shared with me if I had been a little older. If only we had learned *not* to keep secrets. If only we had learned that we could confide in each other.

She must have felt so alone. Sadly, in her diary she made it clear she very much wanted to talk to somebody and wanted to reach out for help about the dilemma she was in, but the biggest reason she couldn't was to protect our family and the church. What would the church people think? It was 1975. What would the church do? How would they react? Would they have been supportive? No! Would they have talked about options, lent her a helping hand or a shoulder to cry on? Most likely our family would have been ushered out of town quietly. History shows—heck, the Bible shows—they would have started looking around for stones to throw at her.

On a brighter note, I have been blessed over the years with pastors who listen and love, who have allowed me to see what a true pastorate looks like and should be. They have offered a caring heart to me in a million different ways at different intervals and points of growth in my life.

From internationally known evangelist James Robison to my megachurch pastor Alan Jackson to my present-day small town pastor Shiloh Hackett—these men have been true examples of spiritual leadership in my life. Each one instructed and taught me. I have heard these words often, "We are *in* this world. But we are not *of* this world." That means learning to navigate both worlds with love and kindness and forgiveness. Not just tolerating and loving others—but doing the same for myself. Forgiving myself meant, at some point, I had to stop suppressing things in my life. I suppressed so much from my past in my performances because I was scared . . . and eventually that led me to depression and rehab.

But first, I killed it at the convention and left Indiana as a star. (NO, no one died. That's comedy talk . . . *I killed!*) Well, I'm pretty sure I was not a star, but I sure started getting phone calls. A lot of phone calls. I started to get calls from church groups throughout the South and Midwest to talk and perform before their groups. They all wanted to hear funny stories about the preacher's kid with the funny voice and the even funnier name.

While other comics were cutting their teeth at open mic nights in comedy clubs around the country, I was cutting my teeth at church gatherings, choir retreats, and pastors conferences. I was trying to tell stories and jokes while learning the differences between a hundred theologies and denominations—and doing it without a two-drink minimum. I should get an HBO special for that alone! Or maybe a Nobel Peace Prize for remembering the differences between the Baptists and the Methodists. One has much better-looking church members. Just kidding!

Then, of course, I had to learn the differences between white churches and black churches. Same God, same Jesus, but very different. A black church will talk back to you. It's not really heckling in a Christian comedy market. More like a rhythm, a banter related to testifying in church. I love it. And I think they loved me once they realized Chonda wasn't the name of a funny black woman.

From Music Row to the church basement, my career was off and running. I could fill hundreds of pages about those early years. My sister-in-law, Doris, traveled with me during those early years. She played the piano, and we would roll into a town in our minivan with a few boxes of cassette tapes and my Bible in hand like a shield. Not in the spiritual sense, but in the "please don't tar and feather me because I'm being funny in church" sense. I was not as much timid as I was nervous my grandmother would show up at anytime with her handbasket.

## CHAPTER 8

# THE THERAPY OF COMEDY

There was really no one particular person in my life from whom I learned to do what I do. My favorite preacher at the time was Dr. Nina Gunter—she was a huge inspiration to me for speaking about spiritual matters, and she was also one of the first female preachers I had ever known. I had watched a few female comics in my life—but no one who took a room from hilarity to heavy to holy. I was blessed to be around a few other women's speakers from time to time—many hilarious speakers and some truly incredible motivational women that steered a room to long more for Jesus. It was on-the-job training at its finest.

I have never considered myself a comedy expert or writer extraordinaire. What I do realize now though was that I had the greatest "tool" in a public speaker's arsenal, but at that time I'm not even sure I realized it. The Holy Spirit. Yes, as cliché as it may seem to you. If you really want to make an impact in any field, you can listen to your managers, agents, teachers—all of them. But first and foremost, listen to the small tender voice of the Holy Spirit.

That on-the-job training led to some pretty remarkable lessons. For instance, on one occasion, I was right in the middle of my joke about the evangelist and the carnal cat. I was about twenty seconds from the punch line when the leader of the group walked on stage and asked if she could borrow my microphone. That is not what usually happens in the middle of a routine, but of course, I handed her the microphone. She paused for a minute, took a deep breath to compose herself, then said, "I have some tragic news. There's been an accident involving a group of ladies on their way here. There is at least one fatality. So, if the other ladies from that group would meet me in the foyer, I will share the details with you."

Then she handed the microphone back to me.

Silence blanketed the room. Sniffles and tears began slowly as the small group gathered their purses and started to ease toward the back door.

Now what? Do I finish the joke? There are no instructions in the *Comedian's Illustrated Handbook* on how to handle the most awkward and serious situations before you finish a joke. So I told my sister-in-law, Doris, to play something on the piano so we could all sing and pray together. That seemed to work. I suggested we take a fifteen-minute break to console ourselves amidst the tragic loss. I went into the ladies' room to think about what I could say to ease the pain and make them laugh.

Then it came to me. I decided I'd go out and say, "All comedians want to kill, but not this way." NO! I did not say that. (I just typed it in case Mom is reading this in heaven because I know she just gasped.) Funny thing, as I was washing my hands in the bathroom, a lady approached me and said, "I don't want to seem insensitive in the midst of tragedy, but what was the end of your story? I'm dying to know what happened to the evangelist's cat."

Right there I realized there was a room full of women who didn't know the deceased—women who had come for a reprieve and for some fun. The show must go on. I stepped back on the stage and began again—timidly and tenderly. Within minutes, we were all laughing, and as I spoke honestly about grief, my sisters, my life—well, it became more than just a laugh—it became comedy therapy.

That church invited me back three months later. This time, the group that had left early was sitting together on the front row. I began by saying, "Now, where was I?" They laughed. Afterward, one of the ladies said the woman who had been killed had a son who was sitting in the back of the auditorium. I walked back and shook his hand. I told him how sorry I was, and he told me his mom was a big fan. I noticed his motorcycle helmet sitting beside him. "Yours?" I asked. He nodded, and I said, "Let's ride!" I am pretty certain he was surprised I actually got on the back of his bike and knew how to lean into the corners. Sweet memory.

Another time, after I had finished a concert, a woman came up to me and asked how she and her husband could get back to church. I was about to make a joke about the two of them just getting in the car and driving there, but something told me not to do it. You know that thing most people have in their brain that stops them from saying something stupid—that thing I don't have? At that one moment, for once in my life, mine worked. I paused, and she started to cry as she told me how her husband had taken their three little boys fishing when their children were four, six, and eight years old. The water got choppy, and the boat capsized. Her husband tried to save one boy, then another, then the third. It was too much for him. All three of their sons drowned. The woman looked at me and said her husband couldn't bear to go back to church because the songs make him too sad.

I had ended my story onstage by making the point that the medicine of laughter had been a great part of my healing and that grief doesn't last forever, but how in the world could I help her through pain like that? It was way above my pay grade.

But in that moment, it hit me that I had seen a desperate face like that before. My mother. Longing for an answer. A validation of her life amidst great pain. Direction. I didn't think, I simply wrapped my arms around her, spoke as kindly as I knew how, and told her the honest opinion from my soul. "He may never be able to go back to that church," I said. "You might find a new place where you can worship without a swirl of tender memories." Then I urged her to find a grief counselor. We cried together and prayed.

I'm telling you that story for a reason. During that season, more and more women came up to me after I finished speaking to talk about tragedies and trauma in their lives. I found that the more I shared about myself, the more they would talk to me. It was like I was giving them permission to open up about their secrets and problems. The more I would lighten the load on my own shoulders, the more they would unburden themselves with long confessions about anger and grief and loss. They looked to me as if I was strong because I was on stage talking about what I had gone through. It gave them hope, and it sparked a mission for me . . . a mission to help, a mission to share hope.

I have laughed often, "I really didn't set out to be a comedian. I just wanted to tell my testimony, and everybody started laughing." There is probably more truth to that than I even realized back then. There are professional definitions for what "comedy" actually is. Most all definitions that I have read talk about the happy ending. In comedy, there is always a laugh at the end. In a comedy movie, there

is always a happy ending. Here, I was unintentionally or intentionally telling and retelling the good, the bad, and the ugly of my life. And yet, there was a happy ending every night. Somehow, the tragedies I had experienced in my life were turned into triumphs. My comedy and confessions were becoming comfort and compassion for others. I was learning to construct a good story or a funny joke, but God was constructing something totally different in me. Even when I had no idea what I was doing, God knew exactly what He was doing. And the one receiving the most healing in the process was me.

However, when it comes to defining comedy, you will find a dozen descriptions and definitions. Many comics will tell you that familiar phrase, "Tragedy plus time equals comedy." For me, comedy plus time equals *relief*. Tragedy just always seems to find me whether I'm laughing or not. Or at least stupidity does!

## CHAPTER 9

# BEING BROKE AND BROKEN

It's quite challenging to go broke if you have no money. You can be broke and poor, but to *go broke*, you have to make money first and then lose it, spend it wrong, make stupid decisions. And that was the Chonda plan in the 1990s.

It all started with bad advice, and boy, did I get that!

I was a working mom. It's the same story for countless other women in my generation who have dreams and ambitions plus a husband and kids. They were and still are the most important people in the world to me. And yet, I began to get pulled and tugged by every phone call and invitation. I thought I was juggling it all well. I also thought I could still fit in a size two dress. To be honest, I don't think I was growing an ego—at least not like some superstar-having-a-tantrum-'cause-someone-stepped-on-my-fancy-evening-gown kind of ego. No, I think I just had no clue how many items I would have to start juggling at once. You know those amazing jugglers—they have not one but three bowling pins going in the air, and then someone tosses in a chain saw! Yes, that was me!

David was supportive. He picked up so much slack at home while I was on the road—preparing meals for the kids (more like ordering the right pizza), taking them to school, doing the laundry (more like *his* laundry). He did his best, and he absolutely loved being with the kids. Many nights in bed when we would go over the details of the day, he would say, "I know most men don't get to be with their kids like I do. I really love taking them to school." But there was no getting around it; money was needed, and I could bring in more than he could. As a result, he put his dream of writing novels on hold and started writing comedy for his wife. He took a course once in a while instead of nonstop classes to get his Master's degree. Looking back, it saddens me—wondering if it made him feel "less than," but I also know for certain that he loved hanging out with the kids. He just loved it.

But no matter how loud and boisterous I had become in my comedy life, this 1990s woman was still a southern girl raised in the '70s who had some old-fashioned views of what women were supposed to be doing. It was confusing for me, as it is for many women. We were told we could have it all, be mother of the year and a CEO, and be great at all of it. Cook a nutritious meal and iron your husband's shirts, and your children will rise up and call you blessed, all while you're running a Fortune 500 company.

Guess what? It doesn't work that way. And it drives me nuts when Hollywood actresses who have four maids, three nannies, two cooks, a personal trainer, and one child give us women in the heartland advice on how to lose weight, be stress free, and live a perfect life. Let me say it bluntly—it was hard for me, and it was hard for most women that I know. I have lost count of how many nights I fell asleep sobbing on the pillow about whether I was neglecting my husband, my children, and my home. I loved my job and was often too afraid to say it. I loved my family and my home and was too sad to tell it. I was the breadwinner, and at that time in culture, it was still very shaky ground for a woman in the Bible Belt. I could bring home the bacon, but I needed to be the one frying it up in the pan and washing the pan when it was done!

When calls began to come in from agents and managers, it was like a gift from heaven. Finally, help was on the way. But here is where the "going broke" comes in. Let me just set it up like this: I did a tour one year that grossed $2,000,000. Yes, that's two million dollars. But because of said managers and agents and drivers and accountants and ten other people with *hands out* ready to *help out*—I took home $25,000. That's 1.25 percent. Read that sentence out loud. And when you do so, please be impressed I did that math all by myself.

I was doing everything backwards. I didn't have a promoter, but I had people around me constantly saying, "We will do better in-house." So my folks sold the tickets, printed the posters, and made the phone calls. We built a network of churches and friends and their friends' churches and friends' networks—and this was all before Facebook existed. I had a bus, an entire band, a manager, and a woman who booked me (the manager's wife). My manager at the time thought perception was everything. Make a big entrance, look like a star. So, I would come into a town with my bus and my band and a semi loaded with production gear, sing three songs, talk for two hours, then leave. My manager told me this is how it was done. And maybe there was something to growing it all. But the bad thing was there were not any other female comics in my genre to learn from or network with. The people around me were making great money and great names for themselves, and I was still having to work twenty-eight days a month to pay all of them.

I think even Colonel Tom Parker would have stood up and said, "Stop, you're ripping off this poor, dumb girl."

I know I was completely naïve, and I really don't think they did it out of bad intent. I really don't. I think they did it because they saw me as something new, something different, something that's never been done like this . . . we were building something, growing something . . . okay, who am I kidding—Chonda was a cash cow. And by the way, I am the only one who is allowed to use the words "Chonda" and "cow" in the same sentence.

And I am embarrassed to admit it, but I have to be truthful: my ego had a little to do with it. I figured since I was attracting big audiences, I needed a big bus. I had all the trappings of a popular artist but didn't have the HBO special. So, as much as I thought we were really "going places," nobody outside of the Christian market knew who I was, which did make for some funny moments. One time I had the same bus driver as Faith Hill. He took one look at me, and I felt a chill, as if he was asking himself, "What did I do wrong to end up with this B-level comic?" He had no clue I was playing to six thousand people per night, be he decided I was a B-level talent—and he treated me like one. If I needed to stop the bus for food at a grocery store, he would park seventy yards away from the front door. When we needed to load boxes in the bay, he insisted guys carry them instead of getting too close to the storage facility. Believe me, if I had been Carrie Underwood, he would have parked on the sidewalk and carried me in, but instead he acted like I had leprosy.

To be fair, if I were a male bus driver, I'd probably want to carry Ms. Underwood in no matter how far from the door, but it was as if he took one look at my rear and thought to himself, "That girl needs to get in her ten thousand steps today. I'll help her out by parking as far away from the door as I can."

After a couple of those incidents, I mentioned to the driver that it would be nice if he could pick me up at the theater door, but he acted like I was working for him! Then one night I finally had it. I had just performed in front of a sold-out crowd where five thousand people had laughed and clapped. I was tired, and sweet Christian words of encouragement were probably not swirling around in my head at the time, because I walked out of the theater and the bus was so far away I couldn't see it. I kept walking in every direction in the parking lot until finally I spotted it. I probably lost two pounds on the hike, so some good came out if it. I marched myself on over, climbed the steps, and declared, "Mr. Driver, can I tell you something? My money is as green as Faith Hill's and Garth Brooks' and I'm paying what Faith and Garth pay, so how about a little respect?" Well, that told him! At the next venue he parked within shouting distance of the theater. The bad news was it was next to a Chick-fil-A, so I put back on the two pounds I had lost in the parking lot the night before.

That was memorable, but my favorite bus driver story happened in Maryland. We were coming out of Baltimore with another driver who somehow was under the impression that I should walk a mile through every parking lot. But this driver was also a combination of Dale Earnhardt Jr. and Kevin Harvick. He couldn't wait to get me to the next venue and watch me walk. So there we were, in the back of the bus, zipping down the highway, and I knew he was going to get pulled over for speeding. Any performer who has ever been on their tour bus can tell. You're going fast, and then all of a sudden you start to slow down. You can feel the rumble strips, hear the gravel, and see the flashing red light. He was busted.

My tour manager went up to see what was going on, and about ten minutes later he came back with a big grin on his face. He was holding one of my CDs, an 8x10 photo of me, and one of my books. He asked me to sign them all to Becky Sue.

I signed them, and for the rest of the trip, that bus driver could not have been nicer or more polite. He treated me like I was a combination of Jennifer Lopez and Queen Elizabeth the Second. What happened was the state trooper was going to bust him good. Speeding. Reckless driving. Doing sixty-nine in a forty-five zone, which sounds dirty. And his logbook wasn't filled out, so he was in T-R-O-U-B-L-E.

As the trooper was getting ready to cite my driver for six hundred violations, he asked, "Who are you driving?"

The driver said, "It's a nobody, some clean comic."

"Who?" asked the officer.

"You won't know her. Nobody knows her."

The trooper insisted.

Finally, the driver said, "Some woman named Pierce."

The trooper went nuts. "Chonda Pierce! Oh, my gosh, she's my wife's all-time favorite comic. In fact, she just saw her the other night and went to buy her CD and book, but they were all sold out. Do you think you could get me an autograph? If you do, I'll let you go with just a warning."

From that day on, I couldn't have had a more conscientious or nicer driver.

I did have to fire one driver. And it was a shame because his driving was fine, and he parked really close to the venue. However, he was a movie fan. Why is that a problem? Because one time after we checked out of the hotel, I was looking at the bill—since everything went on my credit card. He had $400 in charges for one hotel movie! And you can guess what type of movie. He had watched it nineteen times in two days. I didn't fire him for being immoral; I fired him for stupidity, because I probably looked so dumb to my credit card company. They must have thought A) this Christian comedian approves of porn, and B) how could somebody not get the plot of a porn movie the first eighteen times?

I have countless funny stories from the road, but there are others so powerful that they'll stay in my heart forever. I was on my Four Eyes Blonde tour, sponsored by LensCrafters, which I think was the first and only Christian tour they ever sponsored.

A beautiful side story: I was doing my sound check in the theater a few hours before the show while twelve guys in orange jumpsuits—a local prison work release crew—were setting up the seats. Since the event was sponsored by LensCrafters, everything was vision related, so I decided to sing "Mercy Saw Me." The only songs I couldn't sing were "Doctor My Eyes" and "Bette Davis Eyes." And I'm guessing they never sponsored the Stevie Wonder World Tour. But I digress! As I was singing, one by one the prison work crew stopped talking and working and sat down to listen as I sang. "Not what I was but what I could be—that's how mercy saw me."[1] When I finished the song, they jumped up as one, clapping and weeping. That night I performed in front of six thousand people, and it was not nearly as memorable as the reaction I got from those twelve inmates. God let me have that memory, and it will stay with me the rest of my life.

With all the travel, the concerts, singing, all the ups and downs, I didn't take time to keep track of the money that was leaking out faster than a speeding bus driver. After all, that was supposed to be my manager's job, right? Maybe my husband's job? Accountant? Someone lost focus.

To that manager's credit (and I'm pretty sure, if he's reading this, he knows who he is), things started happening fast. Really fast. My VHS projects that soon became DVD projects started flying off bookstore shelves and tables at concerts. We were not only building a career but an artistry that had never been done before. Mark Lowry came close and was a giant support early on. Bill Gaither noticed, and his endorsement was tremendous. But for the most part, what I did—what I still do—was not the norm for Christian speakers, humorists, or stand-up comics. And as the phone started ringing and the offers came rolling in like raindrops, we could barely catch our breath.

Before I knew it, I was paying my manager his fee, his wife a booking fee, and his son a PR fee. Yep, his firm was collecting a total of 52 percent of my income, which only left 48 percent for the

1 "Mercy Saw Me," Geron Davis, *Holy Ground (Live)*, Integrity Music, 2010.

government to take. Finally, I asked the accountant he recommended if she knew an entertainment lawyer who could do an independent analysis of my business dealings. She did, so David and I went to meet with Jeff Biederman (I'm inserting his real name proudly) who took about a minute and a half to look over my contract, assess the conflicts, and say, "Chonda, this is the most unconscionable piece of crap I've seen in my entire legal career." Except he didn't say *crap*.

What a mess! It took some negotiating (that's a nice word for *payoff*), but Jeff got me out of that deal. Sadly, as in many business situations where things go south—what was once a wonderful friendship and family feeling becomes bitter and, well, sad. However, it didn't' stay that way. A few years later, we ran into each other in Estes Park, Colorado. We immediately regretted the heavy feeling between us, and he said, "Sit down here. I want to talk to you." We cried together, talked things through, and reconciled all our differences. We recognized the crazy whirlwind that we both were caught up in. Up to that point in my life, he was the only man who ever sat down and told me he was sorry. And to this day, I attribute him with starting my entire career. My first gold record is because of him. He and David became great fishing pals, and his family is still very near and dear to my heart.

However, there was an underlying problem in me and David. You see, I think David felt guilty that he hadn't realized how one-sided that contract was. With me on the road, he wanted to be the wise hand in my life, guiding me, and David felt he should have spotted what was happening. Ultimately, his feeling that he had let me down was met with my feeling that "no one is watching the store." But that's another story for another chapter.

I realize now that I put expectations on David that he was in no way qualified to meet. At the same time, I felt like he pushed me out the door faster and faster on some weekends. He sent me off to work to bring home the money while he golfed. To his credit, he did spend time with the kids. He knew the names of all their teachers and their friends. But the better he was at being the fun parent, the more I felt resentful, partially from guilt and partially from the fact that I hated being the visiting warden. Bottom line, I missed my kids. I watched Zach play soccer only once. I missed Chera's junior prom. Those regrets still haunt me from time to time. Personally, regret isn't a terrible thing—maybe a regret will keep you from repeating the same mistakes. But holding on to too many regrets—well, that leads to some pretty terrible self-loathing, and THAT you cannot do.

David and I had both learned a few detrimental habits in our childhoods, and we never talked about anything until we were forced to. So, we didn't talk when we were going broke. Having those conversations might have saved us some anguish; but no, we waited until after the fact. It was a pattern with us, like how we didn't talk about Zach's driving habits—we simply waited until after he wrecked the car. We were the poster children for "close the barn door *after* the horse has escaped."

In those days, if Chonda Incorporated were a pie, it would have been an eight-slice pie divided up fifteen ways, and the only one who wouldn't get a piece would be Chonda.

After our meeting with Jeff Biederman (doesn't that sound like the manager in *Some Like It Hot*? Or was his name Beanstock?), he became more than our entertainment lawyer. He was a sounding board, a confidant, and an adviser who assured us that our growing pains were nothing new to those walking this path. He had some big-name clients, and we felt we could trust him, so he went to work cleaning up my financial mess.

While Jeff was untangling the finances, David and I found a better accountant. We slowed down, and we stopped the gravy train that was bleeding our bank account dry. I vowed to go back to doing only my church gigs. Merchandise sales would help us get back on track. Chera's braces would be paid for. Zach could get a better car.

So, I started speaking at just about every Women of Faith Conference in 2001, which is a Christian-based, live-events organization that had twenty-five thousand people attending twenty conferences a year. For almost fifteen years, those weekend conferences became a wonderful opportunity, a chance for me to be unleashed onstage and be completely unashamed of my faith. They helped me realize that I wanted to give women more than a laugh. Don't get me wrong—I want to make people laugh. In the end, that pays the rent. But I also want women to understand that whatever they are going through, I can relate. I want them to not just understand they can survive—I want them to SEE that they can survive. I want to empower them.

As I performed at each live event, I gained the confidence to begin broadening what I was saying to audiences. I went beyond jokes to tell stories that had a point. Right now, you're probably thinking, "How does this ADHD, chaotic, all-over-the-place person ever get to a point?" But onstage, I do. And that led to me recording DVDs with messages about what was going on in my life and what my audience/sisters could learn from that. And guess what? Those resulted in my holding the record for the most certified Gold and Platinum DVDs of any female comic.

Hello, Late Night—I'm waiting by the phone for my Netflix special!

With each of these live events, every time a woman came up to me to thank me afterward, it made me feel that maybe I really could help. Maybe there really was some purpose for the pain of my past. Because oftentimes, women fear their own imperfections in the church—but they weren't afraid to come to me, because they are me and I am them. But let me remind you—I try to help whenever I can, but I'm not a professional. The desire to do more led to the creation of Branches (more on that later) and what I try to do on social media.

Facebook is more than a way for my fans to follow what I'm up to. It has turned out to be a way to stay connected in our struggles together. "You are not alone" is an understatement when you see hundreds of posts about your comments and struggles. Over the past several years, I have received thousands of emails and Facebook messages from women who are desperate, sometimes suicidal, at the end of their rope. They've either read something about me, watched a DVD, or seen me on stage, and they find hope in the fact I'm still standing. They reach out to me with a cry for help . . . they are looking for validation and they want to know they are not the only ones who feel distraught.

In time, I finally found another manager—a pretty good manager. My accountant recommended that David and I talk to Mike Atkins. Given my money problems and my career lull, I was skeptical. At that time, managers had left a bad taste in my mouth. I looked up his information and discovered his reputation was impeccable.

Mike Atkins managed the biggest names in Christian music. He was the man everyone said I needed to meet to get my career back on track, but he was a music manager. How would this work? Later I discovered he had started his management career as a boxing promoter. Perfect! I figured we could slug it out together.

I had no idea why a comedian like me would want to be involved with someone who managed musicians and promoted boxers, but I figured what the heck, everyone is saying I must see him, so why not reach out? I called for an appointment assuming I would hear back in a year. He called back ten minutes later and told me to come in the next morning.

In the meeting with Mike Atkins, he said he and his wife were big fans. Shock! As we talked about my career, he said, "The first thing we need to do is get you off the road." What? The road was my life and my income. I panicked, feeling worried about making enough so the kids could eat, so we would have a roof over our heads, and so the twenty-three people I was supporting would be able to keep taking money from me. Oops, did that last part sound bitter?

Mike told me I had oversaturated the market and was killing myself for little to no money. Too many employees. Too few days with my children. Too little time for what should be my top priority, my husband. Evidently, he had seen this pattern before, and he said, "I can fix this."

Hands shaking, I asked Mike Atkins what his fee was. With what I had been paying my old team, I figured anything less than 98.5 percent for him, 1.5 percent for me was a bargain. Mike said, "I could never take more than Jesus," so we went with 10 percent.

What impressed me most about Mike was not only his ethics, honesty, and integrity, but the fact that he was going to get me out of financial ruin. What sealed the deal was that he was the man who had saved Sandi Patty's career (even though she has mentioned me when talking about saving careers!). In case you don't know of Sandi, she is a Christian singer who was known as "The Voice" before the popular TV show came to be. Angels sit around on high and wish they could sing like Sandi. Well, she may sing like an angel, but Sandi is human; she had gotten divorced and then confessed to an affair with her married backup singer (whom she later married), and that made her an outcast. Because as we all know, we Christians should stone adulterers to death…wait, maybe not. If we did that, we'd run out of stones. Anyway, Mike got Sandi's career out of the pits and back to the top of the mountain, and now he was trying to get me out of my financial ditch and back on solid ground.

For the next five years, Mike created a presence for me in the gospel music world. Promoters took notice, and I started getting booked at better places for a better paycheck. For five years, things were going pretty good for Old Chonda. Okay, not Old Chonda, which sounds like a used car. I can see the ad now:

"Labor Day sale! Stop in at Brennan Motors for a test ride in our used 1960 Chonda."

Mike got me endorsements, he got me into the first tier, and he got me enough money to start building a real life for David and me. I was making enough money that I was able to buy the Funny Farm—almost one hundred acres of rolling hills outside of Nashville where we built a lake and a cabin for tired, burned-out pastors and missionaries. And then, after five years spent rebuilding my career, Mike called one day from a duck blind and said he was retiring. I knew it was a duck blind because A) he said it was, and B) I could hear him call a duck. Either that or he had bad gas. That's a joke, people. We all do it, and passing gas is funny.

Losing Mike Atkins was hard, but he needed to slow his life down, and who could blame him? He'd done an amazing job for so many people, including Point of Grace, 4Him, Wayne Watson, and others. Nevertheless, I knew I wasn't anywhere near retirement, so my business manager asked if she could give it a shot. She had been around for a while, watching the books, and she had started making big plans for me.

She came to me with her first idea saying, "Chonda, I've watched your career for a long time, and my expert advice is you need to be in California so you can be a superstar." Can we say, "dangling carrot"?

Who would fall for that? Me! Hook. Line. And Stinker! And man, did it stink. Every month was one financial disaster after another. First of all, to be a good manager, never forget how to say three important words: "I don't know." Secondly, look for a manager that gets less stars in their eyes than you do—make sure they aren't dreaming the wrong dream for you.

To be fair, I don't think every manager is waiting for the right dysfunctional-ladder-climbing-gonna-change-the-world wannabe entertainer out there to rip off as quickly as possible. I just think some managers get in over their head. They just don't know or are unwilling to say, "I don't know. But let's figure it out together." But somehow in the middle of it all, they do know one thing—how to spend other people's money.

Side note: Before you assume David and I were complete idiots, you have to remember our backstory. We both grew up struggling financially (a gentle way to say, "we grew up poor") and never wanted that for our kids. We overindulged them terribly. We spent money unnecessarily. And frankly, one of the greatest friends I made along the way was Dave Ramsey! He gave me his books for free, and they resonated with us. Also, I operated in a cesspool of guilt. I wasn't the at-home-baking-cookies mom that I thought I should be. And frankly, I felt guilty because I didn't want to be that mom. I felt guilty because I wanted to be . . . well, *me*. But if my kids, if my audience, if anyone really knew *that* person . . . heck, who is that person and how can I be comfortable with her? We would need about ten more chapters. Sigh.

Looking back, it was a complete conflict of interest for your business management office that handles all the money to also manage the moneymaker. Miss Manager-ette thought we needed an apartment in LA and new projects, new photos, new everything that cost a lot of new money. I was too naïve or too weak to stand up for myself and stop the bleeding. So, again, David and I found ourselves midstream in stress and debt.

## CHAPTER 10

# LEARNING LIFE LESSONS THE HARD WAY

The regret of not being better at handling money is as deep as regretting sin. I have confessed that sin to God, but you can never get the waste back. Yes, I have spoken of "going broke," but I have also been poor. I watched my mother sit in a barren kitchen and literally pray for food to appear on the table for her kids. David and I lived for weeks on Costcutter mac-n-cheese. On Sundays, if we had a little extra money, we would cut up hot dogs to add in. (Yum, now I've made myself hungry again.) I nursed each of my children for over eighteen months. Not because I'm a proud La Leche groupie, but because we couldn't afford formula. On the weekends, my babies belched some hot dog-smelling soured milk! As most of the world knows, financial hardship is stressful.

Financial stress in a booming career is not only hard, it's embarrassing—but we were not hungry. Growing tomatoes under a dripping window air conditioner because you don't want to increase the water bill? That's poor. Knowing you can't make another video for your fans because there is not enough money? That's a disappointment. But that is not poor. Standing in line for hours to get that little booklet of food stamps and a four-pound block of cheese? Yeah, that's poor. I've done all those things. I have faked, "I'm really not that hungry," so my husband would not feel guilty eating the last biscuit.

David and I lived in Glasgow, Kentucky, in 1983 for about six months, just after Chera was born. (Simply typing "Glasgow, Kentucky," makes me shiver.) David had a friend who talked him into jumping into a program to become a nursing home administrator, so I resigned at Opryland. I sat across from the general manager, Bob Whitaker, and explained that my husband needed to do this. "I want to be a good wife. So, I need to take our four-month-old daughter and join him. As a Christian, a submissive wife, a co-parent, I need out of my contract." Don't think for a minute I was being some Stepford wife. I think deep down I was wishing he would say, "No. Chonda, I'm sorry, but a signed entertainment contract is a signed contract. You cannot go." I loved my summer job at Opryland! But he didn't say no, so off to Glasgow we went.

I was a stay-at-home mom in Glasgow. No car. No phone. I walked to the corner pay phone to call mom or my brother from time to time—collect, of course. David came home from the nursing home one afternoon and said, "Your brother called me at work today. Go call him back tomorrow." I loaded Chera in her stroller the next day and pushed her to the corner. It was good to hear Mike's voice. With no phone and no TV, it was good to hear anyone's voice!

I missed him and my sister-in-law Doris terribly. He had a fun idea and invited us to Ohio to spend the weekend. "You can sing for us on Sunday at church, and David and I can go golfing." Golfing. That is something you never do on a budget, and David *loved* to golf. As a matter of fact, during our very first Christmas, my friend Patty worked in a warehouse for a golf company. She was able to get an

Arnold Palmer golf bag, maybe scratched a little, maybe missing a zipper on a pocket, but heck, it was Arnold Palmer. I met her in a parking lot, slipped her forty bucks, and snuck the Arnold Palmer bag in the trunk—kind of like a drug deal on *Law and Order*! You would have thought I had given David a private lesson with Arnold Palmer. He was elated. Of course, he had to put his set of yard sale irons and putter in it, but he was stepping up, folks!

But as much as I knew David loved to play golf and would love to show off his new golf bag, when Mike invited us for the weekend of churchgoing, potluck, *and* golf, I had to tell him no. "What? No?" he asked. I began to tear up. "Mike, if we had an extra forty dollars for the gas money to make it there in our Chevette," (Yep! She was still alive then.) "I would buy a box of Pampers and a pack of hot dogs." I told him we had six cloth diapers and no dryer. So, every three hours with a four-month-old, I was washing diapers and hanging them in the breeze, and in-between she wore tea towels. Our child was the only child in the church nursery with a fork and spoon crisscrossed across her bottom. It certainly pulled at the right heartstrings, and Mike said, "Can you walk to Western Union?"

It was a four-mile walk, but for extra hot dogs, I didn't mind. He sent enough money for gas, Pampers, and two packs of hot dogs! When David came home, I had the table set: mac-n-cheese by candlelight, and I had grilled the hot dogs myself. I was so excited to surprise him. He looked a bit skeptical when he walked in. "Are you pregnant?" he asked.

"No!" I laughed. Then I asked, "What is something that you love to do, but rarely do anymore?" (No, his answer was not sex!) Of course, he said, "Golf!" I clapped with glee. I told him Mike had sent money for groceries and gas, and we were headed five hours up the road to eat home cooking (my sister-in-law is the best cook in the country). "Chera can play with her cousins, and *you* can golf!" David sank into his chair. I was dumbfounded. "What's wrong? Aren't you excited?"

He slowly pulled out a crisp fifty-dollar bill. "Where did that come from?" I asked. He said he knew we were running dangerously low on morale and hot dogs. On his lunch break he had gone to a nearby pawn shop and sold his clubs and his Arnold Palmer golf bag. (Yes, just like a movie scene.) I hugged him tenderly. That was David.

I walked to a nearby pay phone the next morning to call my brother and tell him the story, and I think I heard him sniffle on the other end of the phone. He sent more Pampers money, we bought pork chops, and he said, "Get those clubs from the pawn shop!" We had an incredible weekend.

Glasgow and the administrator program turned out to be a bust. After three yard sales, we finally had enough money to pack up the Chevette and get back to Tennessee. Only this time, we had to live with Mother—all three of us in one bedroom. That will motivate a man to answer every "Help Wanted" ad in the newspaper. Before long, we were out on our own and I was begging my way back into Opryland.

Those were hard times, but not impossible times. It was scary, but we were young, and those days built resilience in us. My husband was a hard worker and landed a job at Vanderbilt University as a foreman in the campus maintenance department. He began night classes to earn his Master's degree in English and repaired air conditioners during the day. After I had been at Opryland for about five years, we decided Chera needed a sibling. Interestingly, after Chera was born, I never used birth control again. And wouldn't you know it—try as we might, we could not get pregnant. My doctor was never as anxious as I was. "Just relax, it will happen when you least expect it," he said.

I told him, "I wasn't expecting the first one!" I decided to try making more Sunday roasts.

Getting pregnant with Chera was a complete surprise, completely unplanned, and a complete shock. But Zach? We looked for Zachary, tried for Zachary, made a myriad of roasts hoping for Zachary. And on Chera's first day of first grade, David Zachary "Zach" Pierce made his appearance.

I had been on complete bed rest for six weeks when the doctor finally told me I could do some light housekeeping and take short walks. (What I wouldn't give for *that* to be my doctor's orders today!) I was lounging on the couch late in the afternoon of September 5, 1989, when it suddenly hit me. "I wonder when the last time the vacuum was run in here." (That's probably why I am hesitant to run a vacuum cleaner to this day!) That's all it took. About four passes around the coffee table, and labor started.

Zach was tiny. Six pounds, eight ounces. I had gestational diabetes. My doctor said if I had carried Zach to full term, he would have more than likely weighed over nine pounds. Ouch, my birth canal must have heard that conversation and voted *no*. An epidural was too risky, and after three hours of hard labor, Zach was born.

The night before I was to be discharged, the doctor came to my room and told me Zach would need to stay in the NICU (neonatal care unit) for a while after I went home. I shuffled to the nursery to see my tiny boy. He was hooked up to bells and whistles and tubes and wires. His eyes were covered as he baked in his tiny microwave. I noticed a tiny Post-it note on the outside, placed anonymously. "Chonda and David, I am praying for you and your little guy."

When David and I got in the car without our baby boy, we couldn't even talk. It felt as if I was leaving part of myself behind. We drove in silence for several minutes until David turned on the radio. The song "Somewhere Out There" from the movie *An American Tale* came on, and I began to cry then sob out loud. My husband glanced over at me, then snapped the radio off. "We don't need to hear any of that," he said.

For several weeks after that, I pumped breastmilk and drove to the hospital every day to feed my baby. The doctor, who was an expert in neonatal care and from India, assured me, "I know exactly what he will do. He will get really bad, but then he will get really great." Thirty-three years later, I jokingly remind Zach I'm still waiting for that to happen.

I was ecstatic the day we got to bring Zachary home. He was so tiny, weighing about four pounds. David and Mom and I were very careful when handling him because he seemed so fragile, and my sweet Chera was so tender with him. While he was sleeping in his bassinet in the living room, she dragged her little chair all the way across the room, then ran to her bedroom to get a book. When she sat down beside him with her book in hand, she said, "Mommy, he's not looking at me. I want to read him a story." She was so cute! She was a little mother hen for quite some time after that.

Those were wonderful days. It felt like we were a complete family—a happily married couple with an adorable daughter and a son who would be great someday. I never imagined anything could tear our little family apart . . . until a crack in our foundation appeared.

About four years after Zach came along, David had an *emotional* affair, and naturally, I blamed myself. Why do some women do that? Of course, I know there are two people in a marriage and marriage is not 50/50. Marriage must be 100/100. But me? I immediately assumed something was wrong with me. Was I too busy being a mom?

Or too caught up in building a career? Either way, maybe David felt cheated; and when people feel cheated, they sometimes cheat.

Bottom line, it happened, and it hurt. The man I wanted to believe could never, ever disappoint me, the one I trusted with my body and my life, turned around and did the same thing my father did to my mother. I was devastated.

It started when we met a young couple at church. Let's call them William and Anna. The four of us became good friends, and we often hung out together after church. William and Anna were trying to start a family, and we had long conversations over card games, late-night pizza, and movies together. They became Uncle William and Aunt Anna to my kids. David and William were pals and played softball on the church team. David and Anna even became friends.

During the day when I was on the road and William was at work, David would talk to Anna on the phone. Sometimes they would meet in person. It was all just friends. Nothing wrong with men and women being friends, right? Although Billy Crystal's dialogue with Meg Ryan in *When Harry Met Sally* comes to mind—And no, not the café scene where the older lady says, "I'll have what she's having!" I'm talking about the argument between Harry (Billy Crystal) and Sally (Meg Ryan). Harry infers that a man cannot be friends with a woman that he finds attractive because the guy will always be thinking about having sex with her. Sally says, "So a man can only be 'just friends' with unattractive women." He insists, "No, you pretty much want to nail them too."

Being Sally, I could never imagine anything was going on. Anna was attractive and kind. And she was my close friend too. Occasionally, she rode along with me to concerts. The long bus rides with a friend helped to pass the time, and on those early days, a friend in the minivan keeping me awake was a treat. We laughed together and had meaningful conversations. One time Anna asked, "Chonda do you ever worry that David might not be *the one*?" I reached over and patted her hand. I figured this was coming from some deep sadness because she was struggling to get pregnant. I said, "Anna, of course I do. I'm sure all marriages have those moments. But frankly, he's my husband and this is where commitment comes in. Don't let the devil discourage you about William." She never mentioned it again.

Then one Saturday night, David and I rented a VHS movie from Blockbuster—that shows how long ago it was. David kept looking out the window, clearly not into the flick. I finally stood up and pushed pause. "Honey, you're not watching this. You want to finish it tomorrow?" I asked.

He slipped his head back and sighed deeply, "Chonda, have you ever thought I might not be the one for you or that you're not the one for me?" (I know, same words as Anna—a flashing neon sign I didn't see).

"Everyone thinks that once in a while," I said. "But that's when commitment sets in, and you keep pressing on. Look, I have always known you are not the kind of guy who will bring me flowers or remember my birthday every year, but as long as you don't want to do that for anyone else—we are fine."

There was a long, long awkward pause. This time I should have been hit in the head by the flashing neon sign. And then I said half-jokingly, "You don't want to do that for anyone else, do ya?"

An even longer awkward pause. Then David sat up, cupped his face in his hands, and started crying. "I am so sorry. I just don't know how this happened. It just happened. I really didn't mean for this to happen. But it happened and I think I'm in love with someone else."

My pulse quickened, and I started to hyperventilate. I was utterly taken by surprise. My insides twisted as total shock set in. I walked to the bathroom and threw up. If there was ever a time to be sick to my stomach and not be pregnant, this was it.

David said he never meant for it to happen, but he had fallen in love with another woman. He said they had not had sex but had been intimate. What does that even mean? Whether he meant sharing dreams or kisses, it was all the same, and my heart was shattered. Plus, I didn't believe the no sex part. See *When Harry Met Sally* above.

I panicked. What was I to do? I didn't want to wake our kids. I didn't want him to leave me to raise our two babies by myself. I know every married couple has fights, but this wasn't a fight; it was a deep confession on his part.

But in that moment, I decided he had to leave. I didn't even tell him to return the movie to Blockbuster. I didn't care about the $1.25 late fee. I felt a rising panic much like when you find out you shook hands with someone that was just diagnosed with Covid. You just want to wash your hands over and over—like when the lepers would walk through town in the Bible and someone had to pave the way by carrying incense and yelling, "Unclean. Unclean." Okay, that sounds dramatic. But it is how I felt.

David left and spent the night on a cot in his office. I called my brother Mike in Ohio (Dial Superman 911!) and told him, "Something terrible has happened. This is a mess. I don't know what to do."

I'm sure I said many other very dramatic words, and my brother, who is very used to my flair for the dramatic, kept saying, "Slow down. Take a deep breath, Chonda. Don't do anything crazy. We're getting in the car right now. We will be there in eight hours. But don't do anything."

I remained calm. I will pause while those who know me laugh at the idea of me being calm. In reality, I took every piece of David's clothing in the house and threw it all in the front yard. Then I decided

I had to talk to a woman I trusted, so I called Anna and woke her up. "Oh, Anna, something horrible has happened. David is having an affair. He says he is in love with someone else."

She was quiet at first and then asked, "Is that what he said? He's in love with someone else?"

"Yes! It's terrible. What do I tell the kids?"

"Do you want me to come over and sit with you and the kids?" she asked.

"No, I'm afraid they'll ask too many questions."

Zachary was almost five and Chera was ten, but I could picture the interrogation. "Where's Daddy? What have you done with our daddy?"

After talking to Anna, I called Mom who was making her last rounds at the nursing home where she worked all night. She was so compassionate and tender. She knew my heart was breaking, and she knew what that brokenness felt like.

Then she asked me the tough question. "Honey, do you know who it is?"

"No," I said. "I haven't really thought about that yet. Probably one of the women at David's work. Some harlot on a street corner trying to snare my man."

Then Mom asked, "Honey, I hate to say it, but do you think it might be Anna?"

"Anna? Oh, heavens no, Mother. That would hurt her feelings to hear you ask such a thing. She's my friend and she's a good Christian."

As always, Sherlock Holmes Mom had figured it all out.

Mom said she would come over in the morning to help get the kids off to school. I'm sure the neighbors wondered what kind of yard sale I was having with only men's clothes for sale. I felt numb. Finally, I picked up the phone and called David. Mom's question had been rolling around in my brain. I could hear myself saying these words, "David. Just tell me, right now. Tell me the truth. Is it Anna?"

Dead silence. Then he said, "I swear I never meant for this to happen. Believe me. It doesn't matter who it is. I have ended it all. I promise. Please don't call her."

Betrayal at its worst. Of course I wasn't going to call Anna. Why would you tip off someone you were going to kill? Then I decided a call was better because I don't look good in an orange prison jumpsuit, so I dialed her number. After she said hello, I could tell she had been crying. I was livid. I told her she had five minutes to call William, because in five minutes and one second, I was going to call and tell him everything.

Four minutes, fifty seconds; four minutes, fifty-five seconds passed. At four minutes and fifty-nine seconds, William called me. He was calmer than I was. I don't know how she explained it or what she said, but I needed to know her secret. He didn't throw her clothes anywhere. He spoke as if it was such a sad story. "Hey girl. I'm so sorry you're hurting today. I am so sad this is happening."

Then he said, "You know, I was afraid this was gonna happen. Things were just getting weird."

Apparently, everyone saw the flashing neon warning signs but me. He told me he noticed things like when they would go to the church car wash, if she knew David was going to be there, she would wear a bikini top and cutoff jeans. She insisted on making David's favorite foods and having him eat with them when I was out of town.

It was so strange. My mom could see it coming, William could see it coming, even Stevie Wonder could have seen it coming. But me, I was blind to what was right in front of my eyes.

The four of us met with the pastor at different times. We went through a weird custody battle. Who gets the church? We did. So

Anna and William went somewhere else, and David and I went off to marriage counseling for six months.

Unfortunately, two problems remained, both of which had long-lasting effects. The first was that I began to realize how hard my career had been on David. He would rarely admit it, but I think he was tired of me being the lead singer and him playing the tambourine. He wanted to have his own time. Maybe not in the spotlight, but I think my bank deposits becoming larger than his started getting old.

David worked so hard at his writing, but for every book I had published, his pile of rejection letters grew bigger. Maybe he began to feel stifled and unfulfilled. Without the validation of his work, the wrong person showed up in a bikini top and cutoff jeans to give him validation. After she went away, a new mistress began to emerge—alcohol.

There are so many fingerprints of pain in sin. The devil is just so crafty that way. It's a ripple effect that sometimes you didn't even know was attached to your initial failure. Yes, there are consequences, but sometimes you don't even know they exist until years and years later. You see, our secondary problem in all of this remains even now, like a landmine that was left behind to explode years later. A few months after their affair ended, I came around from the back door at the side of the house one afternoon to see why it was taking Chera so long to come inside after she got off the school bus. She was sitting on the porch with a puzzled expression on her face and little tears streaming down her cheeks. She was reading a letter that Anna had left for me on the porch—a detailed apology about things that no ten-year-old should ever have to know about her parents. Chera was used to getting the mail and opening the letters addressed to me. My daughter looked at me through her tears and said, "Mom, are Daddy and Anna boyfriend and girlfriend?"

I stammered out a reply. "No. Absolutely not. Aunt Anna is just being weird. She thinks she loves Daddy. But your Daddy loves you and Zach and me. Daddy loves your Mommy very, very much. This is just silly stuff." I did what I do best: deflect and distract it all away. David did what he did best: never talk about it again in the hopes that it will all just disappear. It was over. And we really did love each other. It was my truth. It was his truth. It was *the* truth. Honestly, I thought that would be the end of it, but almost twenty years later, we discovered that incident caused the first crack in what became another heart-wrenching split in our family.

Now it's time to remain true to my promise to share all the secrets. Remember, unashamed and unleashed . . . and now unburdened. Truth be told, David was not alone in causing devastating distrust. The dangers and temptations and loneliness of the road are a feeding ground for even the greatest, most iconic Christian artists, especially ones as broken and dysfunctional as I was.

I remember late night conversations on the bus with Sandi Patty or honest chats with Michael English. Difficult conversations with several artists that would honestly tell me the perils of road life and loneliness. You would think that those conversations alone would have been enough to save me from myself. Also, you need to please, please hear me—this is not an excuse, but it is an explanation: Fifteen years of heavy touring makes one so very, very receptive to fan flattery in the blinding of the limelight—even if the spotlight is in a church somewhere. Having people around you that are completely committed to what you do, you begin expecting and hoping for their admiration all while you are susceptible in your loneliness. Without "taking every thought captive," your thoughts can lead to downright lust and desire. In my past, I have fallen for all the kind words and late-night glances, and I have perpetrated some as well. For me, it was a tour manager I became much too close to.

A tour manager is the person who handles all the details of road life. They take care of you, they listen to you, they share your drive and passion and make it all happen on the road. They are most often at your beck and call on the road and, like an idiot, it took me a while to realize that the reason they do it is because you pay them. I think both the artist and the tour manager forget that sometimes.

This tour manager made me feel like I was his number-one priority while David was at home and not getting things done. He was golfing and fishing and leaving nothing in the fridge when I got home. He was eating out and having a great time with the kids. And he was drinking more and more. It became far too easy for me to mix up what was real and what was not. Couple that with the fact that the tour manager and I were together on long bus rides for days at a time. Canceled flights forced delays . . . so much time spent together that a work relationship becomes too personal, and the jokes and fun become forward and flirty. For someone like me with low self-esteem and craving validation, those flirtations seemed real, and I found myself asking the same thing David asked. "Is this the person I am really supposed to be with? Maybe this guy is the one for me?"

David and I sat in a counselor's office to save our broken marriage. One of the last times—it was almost like a light bulb powered on in our brains. FINALLY! We were not ready to give up on "us," but we had simply become too polite with each other. Sure, I would be upset every time I had to leave my kids, but I wouldn't dare say anything to make David feel bad for not coming along. David was so embarrassed at the teasing he got from his golf buddies, "Dude! Wish I had a

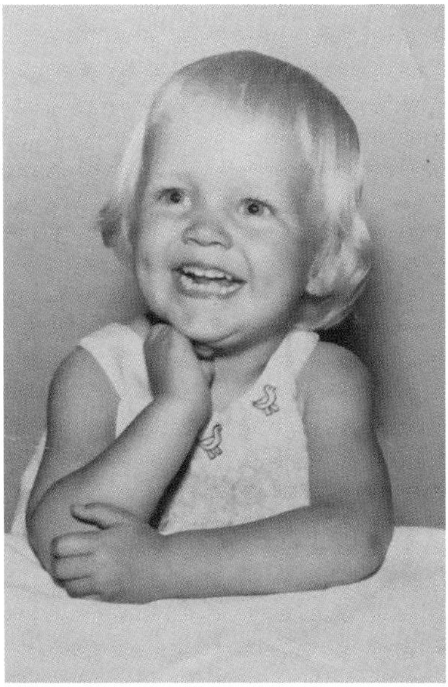

Me, age 3.

Mother asked how she could "cut and paste" my dad out of pictures several years ago. She didn't understand that you could do that on your computer! Not literally "cut" and "paste"! Front row from left to right: Charlotta, Mother, and Mike. Back row from left to right: me and Cheralyn.

At the end of a very difficult day at home. Everyone showed their emotions well—except me! What an actress! Clockwise from top left: Mike, me, Charlotta, and Cheralyn.

August 1978. Mother and I had a giant yard sale to sell as much as possible and leave. I dressed like Raggedy Ann to draw cars to our little yard sale.

Me and David headed to the high school senior banquet, 1978.

Our wedding day, May 14, 1982. Yes, I made my wedding dress!

We got married on the front porch of the farmhouse that belonged to my cousins, Jerry and Ann.

Me as Miss Minnie Pearl at the Opryland USA theme park.

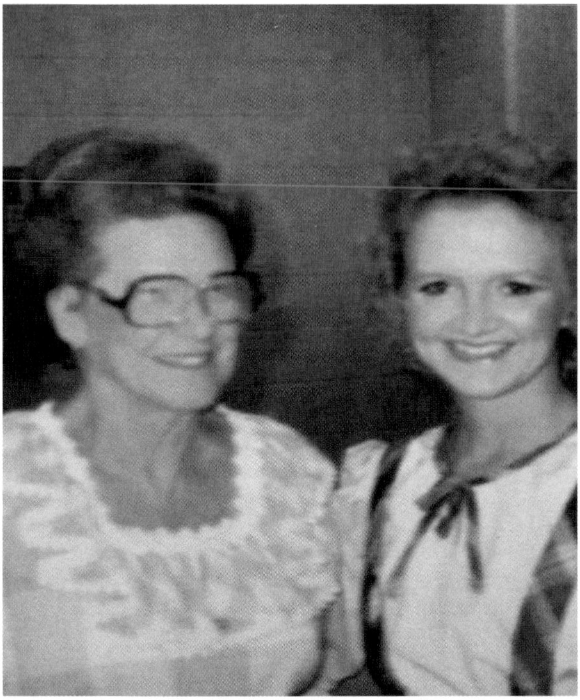

Sarah Cannon, the "real" Cousin Minnie Pearl, and me, August 1986.

Our firstborn, Chera Kay Pierce. She loved climbing at an early age!

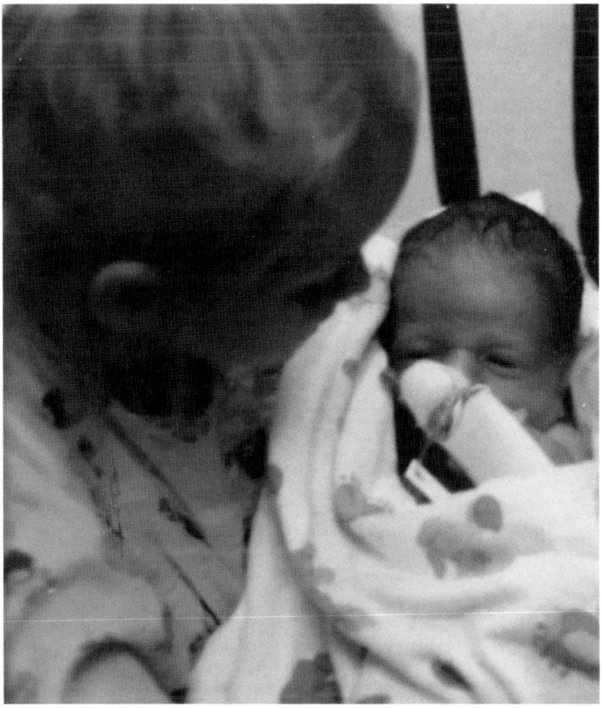

David Zachary Pierce, born on September 6, 1989. He was born too early and stayed in the NICU for several weeks. Big sister Chera was so sweet and gentle with him.

A special event at Opryland USA—the Mayberry Reunion Show. Zach has been my sweetest treasure.

One of our last birthday celebrations with Papaw Sam.

My sweet "adopted" fellas! Bone Hampton, me, Zach, and Drew Williamson.

Our favorite funny man, Mark Lowry.

The love of my life, David Pierce.

David Pierce.

Melanie Vuocolo and me.

Meribeth Maxey LaBearrare and me.

Me and the one and only Judith Hoag.

Glynda Maxey and me.

The Girls of '78:
Top row: Meribeth, Necie, and Mary.
Bottom row: Me, Patrice, and Kim.

Here I am as the Grand Marshal of the Christmas parade in my little town!

Joyce Mayo, my high school drama teacher, visiting the movie set of *Roll with It!*

Andrew Tenenbaum, Nicole and Shiloh Hackett (my pastor), and me.

USO trip to Iraq and Afghanistan.

USO trip to Iraq and Afghanistan. *Photo taken by Mario Barberio.*

Jeff Biederman, me, and Andrew Tenenbaum.

My brother, Mike Courtney, and me.

Me with former Arkansas governor Mike Huckabee.

Garth Brooks and me.

Me and Dr. Billy Graham.

Betty Robison, me, and James Robison.

Me with my mother.

woman to take care of me." But he never said a word. He just seethed inside. And I just quietly became resentful of the pressure.

I was so tired when I came home. The grass needed cutting, I noticed. Little food in the kitchen, I noticed. No flowers or cards to celebrate my birthday. No help sorting the mail. I noticed everything wrong at home. But David noticed more. Maybe because of his experience, he noticed it. I would chatter on and on about how nice the tour manager was, how amazing he was, and what a rock he was for me. I invited him into our lives, remembered his kids' names. I spent more time talking on the phone with him about the next road trip than I did asking David about what he had been up to. No doubt, David could see the flirtation and no doubt, it hurt him. But for the most part, he said nothing. Did nothing. I mean, he hadn't stepped in when the bad eggs on Music Row were groping me; he couldn't save us financially; he couldn't run my tour; he couldn't be the emotional strength I needed. I think it really began to eat away at him—I know it certainly began to eat away at me. Our past ghosts haunted us both.

During one counseling session, David said, "I saw it coming, but I didn't say anything. I think I was enjoying my life too much." What I heard when he said that was, "I left you on your own. I liked my new tractor, golfing every day. I threw you to the wolves . . ." That's what I heard.

But I know David must have felt dejected. My infatuation with my tour manager was a knife to his heart. I really don't think it was some kind of revenge affair. That would have at least sounded more like a bad country song. It wasn't revenge for what he did; I think it was a dangerous spark at a time when I felt completely alone in a marriage that had two people in it. I felt tired, empty, lonely, tempted, and frustrated with a man who would barely remember my birthday. All of that added up to a destructive feeding ground for the devil.

Once again, we foolishly ignored those neon warning signs that were right in front of us. "Oh, if I could go back," I lament often.

Divorce was never on the table for us. The only time I ever used the word divorce was simply to scare David into getting sober. I had gotten wiser about someone I thought I could confide in. When I discovered she was turning around and telling David everything I talked to her about—I leaked it to her intentionally that I had met with an attorney. I even had an attorney friend call David to discuss the farm and dividing assets. I was desperate to see him healthier, and I wanted us together and whole. I wanted to erase our brokenness. I wanted to stop time and undo a myriad of stupid decisions and painful moments in our relationship.

Believe me, in my past, I have had a terrible understanding of boundaries. "I need boundaries" has been thrown around as flippantly as those who touted, "I need space" in the 1960s. I was a young married woman with two kids, and my mother would rarely knock on the door. She would just walk in. On one such occasion, the kids were napping, and David and I were in the living room making a "roast"! Afterwards, I sent her Henry Cloud and John Townsend's book *Boundaries*. It helped a little, but I didn't build an unimpregnable fence around my house. All that to say, I understand the need for boundaries. Sadly, that idea has been stolen to build walls, withhold love, declare some independence with no regard for those learning the concept for the first time. I'm getting better about understanding boundaries and about drawing boundaries around my own life. Much better. At least now I can see most of the flashing neon signs.

In counseling, I learned that broken people attract broken people. I also learned something probably a little more difficult to discuss or understand: that when you are exposed to a sexual act at a young age, you struggle with boundaries for the rest of your life. Something everyone else knows is wrong is part of your day-to-day existence.

My greatest fans! My mother and Papaw Sam.

My daughter's wedding. It was a beautiful day.

The Funny Farm.

Moving day!

Instinctively you know something is evil, wrong, a sin, but when the person you should trust the most says it's okay, well, you go along with it. You cross the boundary; you cross the line and erase it behind you.

This is an embarrassing thing to admit, but maybe someone reading this can understand. You see, early on in my life, I believed that if a man cared about me, it meant he must "want" me. To be blunt, bringing that belief into marriage can be playful at first. David and I had a fun and carefree sex life. But a lack of boundaries and misguided thinking can be dangerous when the honeymoon is over. As the years went by and we began to spend too much time apart, the devil knew exactly where to tempt me. Not knowing how to show love was the biggest danger. When I look back at mistakes I made in the past, I am disgusted at my behavior, my lack of boundaries, and my sins.

It must be one of the reasons the love of God and the grace and forgiveness of Christ is the most powerful love to know. There is nothing more beautiful than to know all is forgiven and forgotten. As Psalm 103:12 says, "as far as the east is from the west, so far has he removed our transgressions from us." Today, I am a different person. I have learned that I don't have to give myself away to express or receive love, which is disappointing to just about everyone on Tinder, 80 percent of the people on Match.com, and 50 percent on ChristianMingle. It's also one of the reasons I rarely date, avoid karaoke, and limit myself to one glass of wine!

Sadly, by the time I realized most of this, when David and I began to understand ourselves better... Well, by the time I could see that I needed to give David more validation (and I am not talking about the Sunday roast), by the time he began to find the freedom to show his skills, by the time we discovered the courage to push through this deep, dark hole of distrust and dysfunction, and by the time we returned to the fullness of our hearts and love again, it was too late. A new word had crept into our vocabulary. One that would overshadow our grief about our pasts, our childhoods, and our dysfunction: *addiction*.

That fight was one we would not win.

## CHAPTER 11

# DON'T JUMP, CHONDA!

Somewhere in all the messiness of life, I crashed. To say I took a nosedive would be an understatement. Imagine your favorite *Looney Tunes* episode with the Road Runner where Wile E. Coyote gets blown up against a wall and slowly slides down to the bottom. That was an easy trip. Mine, not so much. I hit rock bottom with a dramatic *splat*; and that rock bottom meant I was headed up... to rehab.

I should have seen the big dive coming, I suppose. But somewhere between the money coming in and money going out, Chera moving away to college, Zach heading to high school, and David spending most of his time golfing and fishing (did that sound bitter?), I became depressed. I didn't know I was depressed. I didn't sit around crying all the time. I barely had time to sit around at all, and I didn't sleep. I spent three or four nights a week on a bouncing tour bus, and believe me, no matter how fancy you think that is, no matter how incredibly the vehicle is decked out, it is still a rolling, bouncing bed, and unless you take as many drugs as Elvis or Willie, you don't sleep well until the bus is sitting still, and by then you're in the next town for the next show and only have a few hours for a sound check, shower, and then show.

The first sign I was losing it was in Miami. David was out of the country on another scuba diving trip (Bitter, table for one, your table is ready!), and I, along with a few office gals, were going to host a spa weekend in Florida for one Chonda Fan Contest-winner on Super Bowl weekend. The idea was to spend a day at the spa, eat dinner, fly home, and have a half-day of rest before getting back on the bus again.

During dinner, I felt like I had the worst case of indigestion on the planet. I could hardly breathe, and I couldn't stop my hands from shaking. I took some antacid and went to bed. You know that feeling where you need to sleep, and you can't, and that makes you more anxious? I tried to sleep, but my mind was racing with a million things I felt I needed to do and then examining the other million things I was doing wrong. It was like a massive tug-of-war in my brain, and trust me, there wasn't a lot of room in there. In the middle of the night, I decided to take a hot shower, but that didn't help. With the water cascading over me, I began to cry. It was a quiet meltdown, but I was heading toward a Chernobyl-sized one.

I stepped out of the shower, got dressed, and woke one of the gals on the trip—let's call her Martha. "I think something is wrong," I said. "My chest won't stop hurting. I need to go to the hospital, right now."

Martha immediately jumped up and went into Ms. Fix-Everything mode. (Yep. She must be a descendant of Martha in the Bible.) Within minutes, I was headed to the nearest emergency room in Miami. Of course, since I'm kind of a star, they took great care of me (not) and let me lay on the gurney in the hallway for the next five hours. By the time the doctors got to me and ordered a few tests, I had thrown up everything I had eaten for the last month, and I felt crushing pain in my chest every time I took a deep breath.

I was terrified to the point of panic. What if I died? How would David and the kids survive? How would they eat? What if I never got work again? What if a meteor hit Miami that night? Yes, the well-being of mankind was resting on my shoulders, and I was collapsing.

Days later, I was still in the hospital without any kind of diagnosis. Martha and the other girls had to get home to jobs. Luckily, David was passing through Miami coming home from his scuba trip, and as he changed planes, he found our messages and came straight to the hospital. I felt relieved to have him there with me. (You know, after the last chapter—you've got to be reminded. He truly was my best friend, and seeing him in my mind's eye while I type this—well, he always will be.) More tests finally ruled out an impending heart attack, so we decided I should fly home and follow up with my own doctor.

Back in Tennessee, the days drifted by. I didn't want to eat, and when I did, even chicken soup didn't stay down. I was afraid to go back to my pregnancy saffron rice diet, as I'd had my fill of enemas. After a while, I became so dehydrated and weak that my doctor had me admitted to the hospital. I cried a lot and often while the tests continued. Gallbladder? Nope. Heart attack? Nope. Anemia? Nope. Thyroid? Nope.

The tests indicated I had a slight hiatal hernia, and the doctor sent me home with some Nexium (an antacid) and Zoloft. "Zoloft?" I protested. He said it would help me stop crying. It didn't, especially when I saw how much it cost. But the hernia wasn't the main problem. My brain chemistry was out of whack. Something was wrong, and it was all in my head.

My doctor and my new counselor recommended some quiet rest and sunshine. But as soon as I started eating better and the medicine kicked in, they suggested I get back out on the road. Now before you roll your eyes, remember, you are reading these in quick succession. The theory was that getting back into a routine would fool my mind into thinking that everything was just fine. I have said often on stage and in print, "Rehearse in the dark what you learned in the light." It works . . . well, most of the time.

Their advice worked for about a week until one of the rainiest seasons in history began. That is not the best time to be struggling with depression. It rained fifteen days in a row. I spent a few days in sunny Florida trying to climb out of the dark, but it wasn't working. All I wanted to do was curl up in bed and stay there forever. I felt paralyzed by every negative thought of my adult life and haunted by every traumatic childhood memory. Medicine allowed me to eat better, but the crying jags every morning left me exhausted the rest of the day.

Somehow, I could still work, most often at the Women of Faith Conferences. Those gigs were the easy ones for me. Almost all other shows were canceled. I would be backstage crying until the mic was handed to me. I would walk onstage, perform a twenty-five-minute set repeating all the jokes that I knew worked, step off the stage, hand the microphone back to someone, then walk to the green room and fall apart again. I was a walking basket case, and I didn't care who saw me. I stopped every speaker and singer before they went onstage and asked them to pray over me. But nothing worked. Zoloft plus prayer wasn't fixing me. I was hurting and desperate and wanted the pain to stop.

One night I walked into the green room and saw Max Lucado sitting there. If you don't know who Max Lucado is, google him. He has written more books than I've ever read. Okay, wise guy, don't say that means he's only written two! Max is so kind, so pastoral, and his writing is inspirational and exhilarating. He was scheduled to speak that day, and I knew if anyone could talk God into healing me, it would be Max Lucado. Forget Zoloft, I had Lucado! That kind of sounds like the name of a drug you see on late night TV ads.

During a lull in the table conversation in the green room, I approached him. "Mr. Max, I'm depressed. I know I'm dealing with some strange stuff in my head, so would you anoint me and pray for me?"

After a few seconds of silence, as I braced myself for the lightning bolt, he smiled and said, "No need, Chonda. I have watched you pray with just about everyone in this room. God has heard you. Now, we wait on the Lord."

That was it? One of the most prolific Christian leaders in the country said, "No. Wait." What kind of help is that? Looking back, I grin thinking about it. Max was right.

The Bible says, "But they that wait upon the LORD shall renew their strength; they shall mount up with wings as eagles; they shall run, and not be weary; and they shall walk, and not faint" (Isaiah 40:31 KJV).

Not to sound too preachy, but I would be remiss if I didn't stop and make a few points:

In Hebrew, the word for "wait" also means to *hope* for, *expect*, look forward to. Maybe waiting brings hope, or hope helps you wait.

Sometimes it's important to do the right things while you wait. Doing the wrong thing can simply make waiting miserable. Trust me on this!

I hate to wait.

My journey to healing began one weekend when Chera was home from college. She came into my room, sat on the side of my bed, and asked me if she could help me get a shower. I had been in bed a few days, and I think she was really trying to tell me I was starting to smell.

At the time, Chera was studying chemistry and psychology at Auburn University and was preparing to study for the MCAT to get into medical school, so I know she was really trying to help. She asked a second time, "Come on, Mom. Please take a shower?"

I heard her speaking, but I was busy trying to figure out how I could get on the rocks in the backyard and jump in the river. Finally, I mumbled, "I wish I could go to sleep and not wake up ever again. Just help me jump in the river, please."

She didn't respond.

It's funny. Even when you're depressed, you're vain. Depression is pretty self-centered. I told Chera to make sure no one claimed my body or identified me after they found me in the river because I'd be all bloated, and I didn't want anyone to see me like that. I even thought about putting on a couple pairs of Spanx before I jumped so I'd be nice and trim when they pulled me in. Except I then got afraid they would fill with air and I'd float all the way to Alabama like a bloated inner tube.

I imagined the cops' conversation:

Cop #1: "Look, it's the Michelin Man's wife."

Cop #2: "No it's not. That's Chonda. Wow, she's put on weight."

Cop #1: "She's retaining water. Like half the river!"

My daughter did exactly the right thing and went to the living room to tell her dad what I had said. Of course she did. The $46,000 psychology degree I paid for got me a narc with a certificate on the wall. (You know that's a joke, right?)

I was half asleep when David walked into the room. My husband, always practical, always the fix-it man, said, "So, you want to jump in the river *now*?"

"Yes," I sobbed.

Dear, sweet, practical David simply said, "It's not but a couple of feet deep now because they shut down the dam in the winter, and the water level is way down. You jump now and you'll just muddy up your pj's."

Maybe he was suggesting I come back in May and give it my best shot. Plus, the spring fishing would be better while he was looking for my body.

While I contemplated winter temperatures and flow rate and what pj's to wear, David went into the other room to call our pastor. When he told our pastor I wanted to jump in the river, the pastor asked, "Does she know how deep it is?"

The pastor's solution was to come to our house and pray over me, which made him the 3,721st person to do so. He arrived ten minutes later. You may be thinking, "If I'm sick, it takes five days to get a pastor to my house." Well, I'm big on tithing. Trust me. If you bump your 10 percent giving up to 30 or 35 percent, you can probably get a preacher on call 24/7.

So the pastor, David, and I all prayed. They prayed for me to heal; I prayed for deeper water. The pastor anointed me with oil—so much oil that I slid off the toilet onto the floor every time I went to pee.

When everyone realized it was going to take more than prayer and oil, David called my counselor who then called my doctor who then called the cops. Finally, the cops decided I was a danger both to myself and to the local aquatic life. Even worse, it turns out jumping in the river without filing an environmental impact statement is against the law, so David loaded me up and took me to Vanderbilt Psychiatric Hospital.

It was at Vandy that Dr. Michael Murphy looked me in the eye and said, "Chonda, you are clinically depressed."

The only thing that might have been more upsetting is if he had said, "Chonda, you are clinically fat."

If you have never been committed to a psychiatric hospital, a.k.a. the Funny Farm, you should try it sometime (and now you know how the farm got its name). Checking in is a trip, and you can meet some very entertaining people. First, they ask you *not* what your problem is; they ask you for your insurance card (which rarely covers psychiatric visits) and your credit card (they're smart that way). Second, they ask you if you're crazy or if anyone around you is crazy. Then they take you in a little room away from those who brought you in to see if everyone is telling the same story.

While my credit card was processing, they asked about my problems and why I was there. I answered truthfully. "I'm here because the river's not deep enough."

Next, I had to step on the scales. *Why?* Is it a carnival guessing game? Like I wasn't depressed enough, now they're yelling out my weight to fifty strangers. "She's 155!" Evidently, you get depressed per pound.

Everything I came in with was taken from me. I mean *everything.* They took my purse. They took my bra. They took the string on my sweatpants. Okay, I get that. But my hairbrush? Really? Could I brush myself to death? Then, the *pièce de résistance*—the full TSA. They touch both the T and A, and by that, I mean the full body cavity search. The most humiliating strip search you could ever endure. I am so glad I didn't have fiber that morning or too much coffee. And by the way, who in the world hides things there? Did they think I sat at my breakfast table that morning, looked at the butter knife, then said to myself, "I'm gonna hide this up my butt just in case I go to the psychiatric hospital today"?

Once you are weighed, searched, de-butter knifed, and patted down, they give you a blanket and a pillow and send you to a room with a notepad. They tell you to write down anything you are thinking about—but they don't give you a pencil. And I'm supposed to be the crazy one?

Within an hour of walking in the door, I was not only depressed, but I was also terrified. Especially after two orderlies took me by the elbows and walked on each side of me. "Ma'am, you need to come with us now." I have never felt more alone and abandoned in my life. I wasn't thinking about healing. I wasn't thinking about all the Bible verses that could help me get through it all. I was thinking *no one* in my circle, no one in my family, no one I had ever met in my life was there for me when I needed them most. I thought, as quick as a jump in the river would have been, that's just how quickly they pushed me away and out of sight.

While I was being escorted to the padded room, David called Zachary at home and asked him to gather a few things up for me. I can only guess how that call went. "Zach, it's Dad. Listen, Mom's gonna stay in the hospital a while. We are filling out paperwork, and they need you to bring her some clothes because the ones she has on may kill her."

So, Zach packed some "safe" clothes from home. Here is why I love that kid so much. He brought me clean underwear, a toothbrush, and some makeup, the only three allowable items on their "She can't kill herself with eyeliner, can she?" list. Then he added three things on his own: a picture of my family, a Bible, and a T-shirt with a great big, yellow Tweety Bird on the front with the words "Looney Tunes" across the top. On it he attached a tiny Post-it note that said, "Mom, I thought this would be so funny!"

The next day, they introduced me to everyone else on my floor. I met people from all walks of life—young mothers who couldn't cope, men who believed they weren't measuring up to the standards society expected of them, a pastor having a crisis of faith, everyone so dark and struggling, desperate to have the weight of the world lifted off them.

It truly is a weight. If you want to know what it's like, take a heavy weight, the heaviest you can find, and strap it on your head. Leave it there for three days until your neck is so tired you can't hold your head up straight. Put on a pair of sunglasses and wear them twenty-four hours a day. By then, it's exhausting to hold your head up, and there is a dark haze everywhere you look. Then, try to think of every accusatory voice you've heard in your past. Let the incessant negative thoughts and comments keep berating you, tormenting you, reminding you that you're a failure. Tell yourself that you're a bad wife, that you ruined your kids, that if people knew all your dark secrets, they would hate you even more. THAT is depression on a good day.

On a bad day, it's ALL of that and you simply decide you cannot move, you cannot get out of bed, you just want to jump in a river, any river.

And most often, that is all because somehow your brain chemistry got depleted or rewired. You ran out of energy to push back on the sadness, and it began to pile up. The negative voices got louder and louder until the circuit went on overload.

Dr. Murphy told me depression is anger turned inward. I told him that was interesting, but it didn't pertain to me. "I'm not angry. I'm a Christian."

"That's all well and good," he said. "But I am the head of psychiatric medicine of this entire facility, and I say, depression *is* anger turned inward."

I, of course, knew better. "I'm not angry. I'm a comedian. And if you keep telling me that, I'm going to get really angry."

Whoops.

For ten days, I sat in the hospital isolated from my family and friends. On the third day, after talking at length to doctors, therapists, and nurses, I was allowed to make a phone call. I called my brother first. After all, a girl always wants to be rescued by Superman. I tried to be strong, but after a few seconds, my voice weakened. The tears began to flow. I started whispering so the nurses couldn't hear me. "Mike, please, come and get me. Please. Please, come take me home. I will be good. I promise."

Mike's voice cracked and I could tell he was crying, too. "You know I can't do that, Chonda. You're going to learn some things in there. It won't be long. We will talk again tomorrow." That was my one phone call for the day; and for each of the next five days, we repeated the same conversation.

The main activity was group therapy, which I attended four times a day. We sat in a circle listening to others tell their stories. Sometimes the therapist asked a question we each had to answer. "Each one of you, tell the group about something or someone that always makes you smile."

That was an easy one for me to answer. I said, "My son, Zach. At night, when I can't sleep, I ask God to let me see something in my mind while my eyes are closed, and every time, I see Zach. Every time."

Eventually family members were allowed to visit me. David came to see me. I had lunch with my brother in the cafeteria. My family even sat in on some of the depression workshops, which was better entertainment than most TV sitcoms. Then finally, something began to change. Around day nine or ten I began feeling stronger thanks to a new prescription that enabled me to sleep at least four hours a night. The heaviness in my head was subsiding a bit, and I was more engaged in the process. I would walk to the cafeteria eagerly and engage in conversation with others. Even one of the nurses said, "Pierce, you're probably gonna be leaving us soon. You're walking taller!"

I felt hopeful.

Toward the end of my stay, the therapist asked each of us to tell the group about something we had done in our life that few people knew about but which made us proud. I told the group about going to third world countries with my kids on a mission trip to Africa. Even depressed, I was a decent storyteller. Give me an audience, and I can tell a good story. Heck, when I open the refrigerator and the light comes on, I do fifteen minutes. After I finished, I waited for applause, of which there was none. One of the other inmates, I mean patients, a young twenty-something girl said, "Well, I was walking on the beach one day, and I saw a baby shark that had washed up on the sand. So, I knelt and kept swishing water on it so it wouldn't dry out. I was too afraid to pick it up, even if it was little. So, I had to swish the water with my hands until the tide came in and it could swim back out with a wave."

I kept wanting to ask the follow-up question that had to be on everyone's mind: "Did you ever think about kicking it gently back to the deep part?" That is called, "crosstalk" and it is completely illegal in group!

She continued, "But I'm not that proud of that. It will probably grow up and eat some tourist, and it will be all my fault." For some reason, I found that to be the funniest thing I had ever heard in my life, and I busted out laughing.

By the way, laughing at someone's story in a group session is also completely illegal. It's a big no-no when someone is sitting in group with bandages on their wrists from attempting suicide, and now they're even more depressed because you laughed at their most personal story. The head nurse snapped a finger at me and motioned for me to leave group. I moved to a different table alone.

A few minutes later, the nurse walked over, sat down beside me, and lowered her face closer to mine. "Oh my God. When that girl said that, I thought I would bust a gut. That was the funniest thing I've ever heard. Oh, and I'm pretty sure you're gonna be discharged tomorrow. You're laughing again and that's a real good sign."

The next day I was paroled.

I cannot say enough good things about Vanderbilt Psychiatric Hospital. The horrific feelings I had going in melted away thanks to their care and expertise and what I learned during my time there. And believe me, I have told all my dearest friends that the minute they notice me sinking, they need to take me right back. It's been over twenty years since then.

Admittedly, trauma did not make me an expert on depression. Nor did it make me an expert on riparian rights and river depth. However, I am an expert on *my* depression. I am also not an expert on God and faith, but I truly believe one can find complete healing from most anything with a combination of both fact and faith.

Let's alternate between the two.

Fact one: According to the World Health Organization, approximately 300 million people around the world have depression.[1] An estimated 6.7 million adults in the United States have experienced a major depressive episode at some point in the past year. So, I am not alone.

Faith one: The Bible also taught me I am not alone. But it wasn't until I felt I was truly alone at Vanderbilt that I learned to rely on my faith. I needed the stillness of my hospital room with no distractions to make me realize I either had to choose to believe it all, that God was with me, or believe in nothing. "As I was with Moses, so I will be with you; I will never leave you nor forsake you" (Joshua 1:5).

---

1 "Depressive Disorder (Depression)," World Health Organization, March 31, 2023, https://www.who.int/news-room/fact-sheets/detail/depression.

Fact two: Adrenaline is not always your friend. You wonder why you are dragging on Monday after screaming your head off at the football game on Sunday? Or after the euphoria of your favorite rock concert or comedy night? After the spiritual high of the most moving Pentecostal throw down at church? There's a lot of adrenaline involved in those moments. No matter how satisfying, how spiritual, how motivating, we're all prone to have some dark days. What goes up must come down.

Remember that and don't beat yourself up if you're dragging anchor on Monday! Just get some rest.

Faith two: Jesus Christ knew the value of rest when he said to His disciples, "Come with me by yourselves to a quiet place and get some rest" (Mark 6:31). Or as my pastor, Shiloh Hackett, puts it in much more practical terms, "Be like Jesus. Take a nap!"

Fact three: Quoting my friend Dr. Murphy, depression really *is* anger turned inward. My interpretation: get the inward *out* and move on. There is something powerful about hearing your own voice speak the truth. *All* the truth. Not just the comfortable parts, not just the appeasing parts. Find someone you can pour it all out to. I have two outlets: all of you and my incredible therapist, Tracey Robinson, who knows more about me than I could even begin to include in this book. That says *a lot*. She has brought more healing and insight to the voices in my head. I remember lamenting to her during one session how I should have been home, should have been a better wife, should have been a better mom, should have been funnier, should have been thinner, should have been . . . She stopped me and said, "Chonda, you 'should' all over yourself! Stop that!" And we both laughed.

Bottom line, therapists have amazing insights. They notice things, speak things that no other girlfriend, confidant, or family member can comprehend or say. Find one.

Faith three: If you don't have faith, get some. What do you believe in? The Big Cheese. A Higher Power. The Almighty Dollar. The Great Light. The Great Pumpkin. Unless you believe in something—anything—then a conversation about faith is futile. But if you have the capacity to believe in something, then you have the capacity to have faith.

I was taught (poorly) that if I questioned my faith, I would go to hell in a handbasket. What does that mean anyway? Hell in a handbasket? Seems like a stupid mode of transportation to me. Wouldn't an Uber be more practical? Even a Bird Scooter makes more sense. But I digress.

Depression gave me an excuse and a privilege to question everything, and that was the beginning of healing in my life. I got back to faith like King David when he cried out, "My soul is weary with sorrow; strengthen me according to your word" (Psalm 119:28), and when I relied on God, true healing began.

People who are depressed need great counselors who have book wisdom and facts, but we also need the Bible and faith and the guidance of both to give us the strength to face those facts. Facts are facts, but faith? Faith is a choice. Decide and then mark the date and time on your calendar to remind yourself—I CHOOSE FAITH IN GOD.

When I began to question everything about my faith, my questioning became the purging and cleansing I needed. Pour it all out. Lance the boil. Get the hurt, the anger, the sin, the crap all out on the table and start over. I did that by writing down everything I was feeling: my guilt over being away from home too much, my feeling like a victim, my belief that no one really knew me, and the hurt from thinking no one truly loved me.

I addressed each negative thought and emotion by going to the Bible, and it reminded me that each of us are "fearfully and wonderfully made" (Psalm 149:14). I'm pretty sure menopause is the fearful part; and maybe cosmetic surgeons can lend a hand to enhance the wonderful parts you aren't that fond of. But, in my opinion, you can't fight the demons in your mind without the power and Word of God.

Consequently, I am here today because of the power of God, the healing of Jesus, and 150 milligrams of Effexor. That's right, the meds help. Like my glass of wine after a show, the only way you will get that pill from my hand is to pry it from my cold, dead fingers. Please don't come to me citing scripture verses on how prescription drugs are evil. Jesus used *mud* to fill a man's eye sockets so he could see. So until God tells my doctor to stop writing prescriptions, I'm taking my Effexor. Last time I checked, it was, "Thou shalt not commit murder," not "Thou shalt not take Effexor."

I told that story once on stage, and a holier-than-thou lady came up to me after the show to lecture me. "You shouldn't talk about prescription medications. It makes your faith look weak," she said.

I looked her in the eye as tenderly as possible and said, "Then you should take your glasses off and drive home without them." She declined to do so. Carrie Underwood might sing "Jesus, Take the Wheel," but I still want the drivers around me on the interstate to wear their glasses.

When I'm on stage or before a church group, I talk about antidepressants and my sins and the need for the church to be open and compassionate to all. My reason for that can be summed up in a story.

I was with a group of women at a very fancy country club. We were outside in front of the tennis courts on a beautiful afternoon to have a few laughs. While we sat and watched the tennis match, two dogs stepped between the bleachers and the junior tennis match taking place. I'm guessing it wasn't their first date because they were busy trying to make some puppies. They must have met on Tinder. It was unavoidable to see and even more unavoidable to hear. No one in the group said a word. No one moved. Most strained to glance away. Some tried to sit up taller to look over this little *National Geographic* pornographic moment. Grown women were working so hard to pretend this was not happening. Finally, I stood up and pointed out what everybody was pretending not to notice. I shouted loudly to the dogs to break up the mood, gave them a slight kick with my toe, and sat back down. One of the high society debutants whispered behind me, "Thank you." It sounds silly—but I think it was a personal illustration to myself.

Why do we avoid the obvious? Why do we keep trying to look over the unpleasant sights and avoid doing something about it? Why not call it what it is and alert those around us to just stop and go the other way? Maybe it's just me. But there is a reason I am determined to point out the obvious about medication and depression—about a lot of things in my life. Right or wrong—leave it to the comics to point out the obvious. In fact, when I die, I want my tombstone to say, "There were a lot of elephants in the room, and she talked about them."

## CHAPTER 12

# DEEPLY BROKEN IS WORSE THAN GOING BROKE . . . AGAIN!

I mentioned Mike Atkins earlier. He must have done a stellar job putting my finances back together because it took another manager several years to tear them down again. I know, I know—it sounds like the second verse of really bad song. And it is. It is hard to speak of these things. But these "things" are just that—things. My life, my career has never been about money, and I am not assigning blame to anyone (well, almost anyone), but maybe these ridiculous moments in my past can become not just a warning sign for you, but a beacon. Like a lighthouse illuminating before the ship crashes. It must be obvious by now which areas in our lives we had not yet learned to relinquish to God. Yes, ultimately it was my fault. Or David's fault. Maybe both. I'd like to think it was just crappy luck, but the truth is, once again, we did not mind the store very well.

Now before you shut the book and call me stupid—which is my new accountant's job, not yours—I don't think we lived beyond our means. Believe me, my wooded acreage and mortgage look nothing like Amy Grant's ranch. Our first house in 1984 cost $29,000. We borrowed the $500 down-payment from my mom for our two-bedroom, one-bathroom house that was less than one thousand square feet. Our mortgage was less than $400 per month.

Our second house three blocks away from house #1 cost $69,000. Interest rates were horrendous, and in 1989 those payments were $620 per month. That was a pretty big jump for us, but we managed well. Or at least well enough until I quit my job on Music Row. But as my career seemed to be moving forward, we were ready to afford three whole bedrooms. The kids each had their own room, and they enjoyed playing in the giant backyard.

Then came the big move to Murfreesboro. We bought a beautiful 2,400-square-foot home in a nice neighborhood. We lived there for more than fifteen years. If you ask Zach about his childhood home, he will beam and tell you about the house on Comer Circle.

Our last house was 3,500 square feet and located on the Stoney River. We watched it being built and moved in just before Chera went to college. It was close to the high school, which made Zach mad. That poor kid had dreamed about being able to drive to school. His new high school was exactly fifty yards away, across the street; so, of course, we made him walk. For people from Los Angeles reading this, walking is what people around the rest of the country do. It involves using both feet to propel yourself across distances shorter than three miles in temperatures between 15 and 100 degrees. For a while, I loved that house.

Having Zach's school right across from our house was a double-edged sword. I'd be working at home writing comedy, and around noon, I'd hear the door open. I'd go down to check it out and find Zach already flopped down on the couch saying he didn't like what they had for lunch at school, so he snuck out and could I make him a sandwich? The principal usually saw Zach leave and gave him detention the minute he tried to sneak back in.

Eventually, we lost that house. Yes, it was a mixture of poor management, inflation, and frankly—when my family life began to unravel—it held too many memories, both good and bad. One of the poor business deals was the DVD project called *This Ain't Prettyville.* My new manager at the time was also the accountant, and we were guided by people who were . . . how should I put this nicely . . . *clueless.* She had set up a deal where I had to pay the person who helped me write the project a portion of the proceeds for every DVD sold—at a ridiculous percentage.

The manager/accountant didn't account (which raises the question: what part of *accountant* should be accountable?) for the fact that if the store sold the DVD at a discount (which is what stores do to move stock), that I would lose theirty-two cents for every one sold. In other words, the more successful I was, the more money I lost; and the worse it did, the better off I was. It was a DVD version of *The Producers.* I was losing so much money, I would go into stores and hide it so people wouldn't buy it. Think about it. I paid for a writer to help write a few scenes, I paid for production, and I paid and paid and paid when each DVD sold. It was not a good business model.

My so-called used-to-keep-the-books-so-let-me-manage-you manager also had me rent a place in Hollywood. Why? Because I needed a show business address to make it big. Really? Jason Aldean has somehow managed to be okay with only a Nashville address. She was convinced I had to spend more time in Los Angeles if I was going to make a name for myself in the comedy world.

Yes, I could have said no. I didn't. (Insert regret number 327.) At that time in my life, my judgement was a wreck—a disastrous wreck. I have no one but myself to blame for a lot of poor choices. And if I'm perfectly honest, having a little place to hide away in LA sounded good to me. Because where was David? Well, that was the question of the week. Of the month. And of the past few years.

Honestly, we had drifted. Somewhere between trying to give our kids a perfect life, between over-indulging him with things that might make up for what wasn't happening for his career, between him enabling me more than speaking up, between caring too much about building a career to . . . yep . . . we lost each other in the "betweens." We didn't know each other in the "betweens." Between trips on the bus, we needed to cling to each other. Between recording projects, we needed to clear the books. Between managers, we need more prayer. Between . . . well—the vast space of the "between"—we lost each other. That was our biggest failure.

All this made me realize I needed a change; I wanted a change. Something had to change, or I would just throw my hands up and quit. Admittedly, I am a slow learner, but eventually it dawned on me *again* that something just didn't seem right about this *Prettyville* ordeal. I was having one of those lawyer/counselor moments with Jeff Biederman. I'm pretty sure at some point in my career I will get an invoice for all the marriage counseling, life-coaching, and tissues he has provided me over the past twenty years.

Jeff said, "Chonda, I want to introduce you to a manager in Beverly Hills. I think it's time. I don't know if he would take you on, but he could give you an overall assessment of what you need to do next. His firm, MBST, manages the careers of some of the biggest names in comedy. If I set up a dinner meeting with him, would you talk to him?"

I think I laughed out loud. For one, I was so tired, so weary of doing everything wrong, that I was almost embarrassed to have one more person peer into my business. Second, what I do is *nothing* like what the "real" comics do. Honestly, I didn't even know what I do! I only knew that what I was doing on stage was working, but everything else in my life was falling apart. Despite my reservations, I gave Biederman the go-ahead to set up a meeting to meet Andrew Tenenbaum.

A week later, Zach and I sat at a fancy dinner table in Los Angeles when Andrew walked in. He was late. He apologized again and again and told us he had just come from a funeral for his bookkeeper's mother. At least, he thought it was. But he then told us his Spanish was not very good, and halfway through the ceremony, he discovered he was at the wrong funeral. Well, that simply closed the deal. He must take me on! I needed at least twenty years with this guy to hear all his behind-the-scenes Hollywood stories.

Over dinner we talked about my craft and career. He said he had done his research. He found my book *Laughing in the Dark* and said it made a great impact on himself and his wife. She had been struggling with depression. We talked about a million lessons I learned from laughing in the dark. And he said I was funny. Really funny.

He said, "Chonda, I'm Jewish. I don't get the whole preacher's kid material. But you deliver the stories and they're funny. We have got to get you into the clubs. What are you doing tomorrow night?"

It sounded like we were off and running, but "getting into the clubs"? That was about as foreign to me as a bar mitzvah. When Andrew asked me which clubs I had done lately, I thought for a minute and said, "You mean club sandwiches? Um, I did the Birmingham Country Club once. They were having a ladies' luncheon, and I was the entertainment."

I was serious. He didn't laugh. I think he was starting to understand he had just taken on a problem child. His traditional way of dealing with comedians was not going to work with me. I mean, think of me in a comedy club, an older version of Mrs. Maisel. A shiksa version. For non-Jews reading this, a shiksa is a beautiful, gentile blonde that many Jewish men fantasize about dating. Okay, out of the beautiful, gentile blonde part, maybe I'm just blonde and gentile, and Miss Sadie at the Ashland City Beauty Depot would disagree with the blonde part.

I could get up and talk on any stage in the world and make people laugh, but a comedy club? Setlists? Drunks in the audience? Even with my success on my own circuit, I would be the fifteenth comic in the lineup at 1:00 a.m. and no one would be listening. But knowing the comedy club scene is the training ground and launching pad for just about every big-name comic, sitcom actor, or talk-show host in America, I decided to try it anyway.

Producers, directors, and managers drop in at the Laugh Factory, the Comedy Store, and the Improv, hoping to spot the newest talent. Most of the comedians there need to be cleaned up for prime time. Others can head straight to Comedy Central or HBO. But it all starts with a few minutes of a set in a dark comedy club somewhere in Los Angeles, which means a couple nights later, I was standing on a stage in LA doing eight minutes, and it was the hardest thing I've ever done in my career. Maybe in my life. Not the part about standing in a comedy club but talking for only eight minutes. I hadn't done that since I was four.

I didn't "kill" as they say in the clubs. I'm pretty sure the thirty-two people sitting at the bar that night don't remember I was ever there. It was less than memorable, but I did it.

Andrew called a few weeks later. "I'm going to arrange for some folks to come see you. There's a place down the street. It's not really a comedy club per se, but a lot of the big names like Leno and Ferguson pop in from time to time to work on new stuff before going on live TV. So bring your cell phone. You'll enjoy getting some pictures."

I was nervous. Really nervous. It was about the fourth comedy club I had ever entered in my whole life, and I was supposed to be funny in front of Leno? I called David back in Tennessee, and he was kind of encouraging, but he didn't seem all that enthused about it. We had been struggling lately in our relationship. My fifteen years on the road, my depression, his insecurities, and the three hundred other things that crop up in every marriage made it hard for him to be the cheerleader he had been at the beginning of our journey.

That night I took a cab to the joint to meet Andrew. And when I say *joint*, I mean it. It was a strip joint! And there I stood in the back of the room staring at the brass pole in the middle of the stage. No handbasket to hell for me, this would be a one-way limo ride straight to the fiery pit. I was sweating like a glass of iced tea in the Tennessee summer heat. What if someone asked me to pole dance? From what I hear, they don't let you keep your Spanx on.

I watched as a comic scheduled before me took the mic. He was supposedly the next big thing because he had an HBO special coming up, and he was practicing his bits. The truckers in the front row laughed, the cocktail waitresses laughed, the show business executives in the back of the room laughed.

But not me.

I have no words to tell you point-blank what his jokes were about, and I've been somewhat edgy in this book. But when it comes to stories about Jesus, when someone makes comedy out of the crucifixion or tells the most degrading things about Christ and His disciples and their alleged homosexual relationships? Call me a prude all day long. I have a line. And *that* is it. With tears in my eyes, I leaned across the table and said, "I appreciate this opportunity, Andrew. But I don't think I'm cut out for this. I am going to have to leave. I just can't stay here." Then I walked out and never went back to a comedy club.

I look back on that as a very defining moment in my career. Sometimes I think I should have handled it differently. That I should have stood my ground. I should have sharpened my chops and been funnier than anyone in the room. Maybe I should have heckled him. Maybe I should have been bold. But there I go again, "shoulding" on myself.

It seemed like that would be the end of my time with Mr. Andrew Tenenbaum and the end of any advancement in the comedy world. Nope. Before my plane touched down back in Tennessee, Andrew called. He was apologetic about "the loser" on stage. And then he asked to come see me do my thing where I do my thing. He wanted to watch me in a home game, meet my family, and learn about the market I'd been in for fifteen years. Sounded great! Andrew decided to come to my house, meet David, and take in a two-hour Chonda concert at the First Baptist Church in downtown Nashville, Tennessee.

Here is how the script would read in the movie scene about this moment:

> INTERIOR: First Baptist Church
> Two thousand women are lined up and down the sidewalk waiting to get in. Chonda Pierce's new hotshot Hollywood Jewish manager is sitting in the back row taking it all in. He is the ultimate fish out of Hollywood Evian water. He looks scared. Very scared.

After Andrew got over his culture shock, he was very complimentary, but he knew the biggest test was yet to come. He had to meet Mom, who was in the front row. When the show was over, I walked Andrew over to her. "Mom, this is Mr. Tenenbaum. He's the Jewish man I was talking to you about."

Have you ever met anyone who meets someone from another country, skin color, or ethnicity, and suddenly, they think they must talk louder to be understood? That was my mom. Even if the person spoke perfect English, she would talk as loud as she could, slowly and deliberately. She pulled Andrew into a southern bear-hug and at 120 decibels and about nineteen words per minute said, "We love your people. Honey, my church supports Israel, and don't forget, my Lord Himself was also a Jewish fella about your age!"

Andrew just grinned and said, "Yes, and I understand things didn't go too well for Him." I knew right then and there I had finally found "The One." He really is one of the Chosen People, and I chose him.

Over the next few months, Andrew spent his time calling everyone who had been scheming, skimming, and dipping into my bank accounts and read them the riot act to get me back on my financial feet. He told the DVD writer we needed to redo the *This Ain't Prettyville* deal because every time one sold, I lost money. He explained to the writer that there was no choice, we couldn't pay him anymore, and we would have to take the DVD out of circulation unless we changed the arrangement. The writer, not understanding the concept of "you're only hurting yourself," said no. So, we took *This Ain't Prettyville* out of circulation. If you happen to have one, it's a collector's item. If you don't have one and somehow find it in a store and want to buy it, please don't. It's cheaper for me to call you and perform the entire DVD for you over the phone.

To make money, I had to put one dream aside. When I was young, I had dreamed of going on *The Tonight Show* with Johnny Carson and later with Jay Leno. The comedy clubs were the route to that, and they were now officially closed for me. By the way, I finally met Jay in April of 2019, and he could not have been funnier onstage or nicer backstage. But since he had been off the air for five years, it was a little late for me to get a spot on his show.

Back in 2009, my new dream was one I could achieve: To work hard doing what I do and to perform as often as I could and in as many places as I could, not just to revitalize my career but to simply and honestly make the best living I could while focusing on my debt, my family, and nothing else. And thanks to Andrew, we stopped the financial bleeding, and I went back on the road.

It was amazing. Andrew called after I got home from the first part of my tour. "Are you sitting down?" he asked. "You actually made money this time!" Wow, just like a real comedian.

In addition to Andrew, the other good news in 2010 was that my meds were working well, and even though the river was high, there was no danger of me jumping in. But there always seems to be bad news with good news, and on the bad side, David had started drinking again. A lot. And every time we managed to convince him to go into rehab, it cost us $40,000.

I had written a series of $50,000 checks as part of the stupid DVD deal, I was writing $40,000 checks to rehab centers, and I was writing checks for any amount I could to get Branches started. (Branches Counseling Center. More on that later.) Plus, I was paying rent on a fancy California condo to help me get the ball rolling in Hollywood. Plus, I needed a publicist to give me a whole new press look. And then there was Zach. He decided to launch a career in LA, but he needed some seed money to start his ball rolling. Then, Andrew insisted (he was right) that I needed someone to audit all the books and make sure David and I were okay. We weren't.

I was trying to pay back the ruthless producers and writers, fund a few rehab centers, fund Zach. Oh wait, I forgot, *Clueless* (the manager, not the movie) had charged my daughter's entire wedding to my credit card without my knowledge. I thought the wedding had been completely paid for until Andrew called one morning.

"Hey, Mrs. P, we need to chat this morning," he said.

"Okay, great. What's up? *The Tonight Show* finally call for me?" I laughed.

"No. I just got off the phone with your new business manager. She's great. She's uncovered quite the mess. But we're getting it all straightened out. She wanted me to give you the news. Um . . . how do I put this?" Andrew paused. "You're completely broke."

"Again?" I said.

"You mean this has happened before?" I could hear him scratching his head.

Let me tell you, I have had some tough truths to face in this book, serious and harsh realities in my past that I have shared with sincerity. But this stuff... well, to see it in print is just excruciatingly embarrassing. What is my problem? Before you answer that, I will confess I know what a lot of my problem is: I don't say no. I don't rock the boat, or I don't survive. But that's not what I hate most about myself. What I hate most is that almost-debilitating condition my brother calls, "The Disease to Please." I despise it. Although it seems loving to bend over backward and exhaust yourself to give your family anything and everything they want, that behavior is not healthy. Being on the road so much made me feel tremendously guilty and was much of the drive to "make up" for anything lacking in their lives. When David's writing career was moving at a slow pace, I would simply shower him with "stuff." I would try to make up for it with new golf clubs, a scuba trip, or anything that would hopefully make him happier. His wish list for the Funny Farm: a new tractor, a fence needing repair, etc., grew longer and longer. Having grown up with food stamps and government cheese, I wanted to make up for it with my kids. It didn't matter what college they wanted to go to or decided to drop out of, I said yes. I did not know how to allow them to feel uncomfortable. I did not know how to say, "No, I can't do that, pay that, go to that." I'm Ado Annie, I just can't say no.

One of the problems, in addition to my desire to please, was I thought I had the money. My previous manager led us to believe that everything she was doing was turning to gold. She constantly told us things were better than they were. Need a new car? You got it. Chera wants a big wedding? Not a problem. Meanwhile, she was buying a place in France and opening a new office in California. But hey, who wouldn't want an extravagant wedding for their daughter? And who could say no to a son who was truly passionate about something in his life? It's in our human DNA to give our kids everything we never had.

My daughter's wedding dress cost more than my first car. And a wedding dress is only worn once, unless you're Angelina Jolie. The appetizers for her wedding cost more than my old Chevette, although that's not saying much. Of course, since it was a Tennessee wedding, we had the country band and the dance floor, and we didn't go cheap on the possum fritters. I'm kidding, no angry tweets from the Tennessee Chamber of Commerce, please.

Funny, it's not like we were bribing people to get our kids into Harvard. If you had driven by my house and then driven by the homes of the biggest names in Christian music, much less country music, you would never guess I was ever in the same league. Mainly because I wasn't!

Maybe in some small way, I was trying to make up for that. Did I believe my own hype? Not really. I think I just believed everyone else's hype. Maybe I started to believe that to be successful, you must look successful. There are so many things I wish I could go back and change.

Years and years ago, the first of many disastrous managers sat me down in his office and said very convincingly, "Chonda, you have an opportunity to do some amazing things. You are funny. The phone is ringing. You need to get out there and make the most of every single moment. Stop worrying about being gone so much. Your kids and David will bounce back. Listen, your kids will be more excited about the new car you can buy them than they will ever care about you making it to the school play or a soccer game."

Like an idiot, I believed him.

So there I was, in debt up to my assets. Money was coming in from the tour and the bleeding was stopping, but there was still so much debt. The smart thing for us to do was also a very difficult thing to do. We sold the house.

There was another reason to let the house go. David and I both agreed that although the house was filled with beautiful memories at that time—there was that elephant in the room. We felt like those memories were overwhelmingly painful. So we sold the house because the payments *and* the memories were killing us.

Our dream house had become more like a house of old dreams. Broken dreams. A house once filled with laughter and love and excitement was now vast and lonely. On top of that, as I began to pour through drawers and pack boxes, I'd find either a dozen unopened, unpaid bills or a dozen empty beer bottles because David had simply checked out of our marriage and out of life. Despite finally selling a book, he spiraled deeper. Every time I left the house to make some money to keep us afloat, there was a fuss. He was jealous, I was resentful and tired, and we both had our reasons.

David and I began living separate lives at that point. When I wasn't on the road away from him, I was busy packing things to put them in storage. I couldn't bear to have another yard sale, plus I no longer fit in my Raggedy Ann costume. I moved to a tiny 900-square-foot apartment in Nashville so we could stage the house for sale and be out of the way for good. David camped out in our cabin in the woods on the Funny Farm, which was the only possession actually paid for. We bought the cabin years earlier when times were flush—as opposed to us flushing our money down the toilet.

Why separate locations? My counselor and my pastor at the time called it tough love. Since rehab wasn't working and David needed to dry himself out, they made it clear I had to stop enabling him. What's the phrase? When you're stuck in a hole, stop digging. So we threw away the shovel and began to work on our lives.

We managed to make ends meet by selling timber on the land, but I knew that for the most part, it was going to be up to me to save us financially. I was a middle-aged dysfunctional woman with an alcoholic husband, a mountain of debt, a son struggling to get his start in California, a dying mother (more on that later), and that other "elephant in the room."

While the house was up for sale, I was living in an apartment that was basically a large closet. It was so small I could sit on the toilet, fold laundry, and make a grilled cheese sandwich all at the same time. When the loneliness became too crushing, all I had to do was open the patio door and hear life on the streets. Plus, it was only three miles from my mother, who was dying in a hospital across town.

How did I cope with all this pressure? Was it my preacher? Was it counseling? Was it increasing my meds? Nope, it was a karaoke bar in Nashville. Shocking, isn't it?

Now, before my churchy friends excommunicate me, let me say three things about that:

1. I will be the first to admit—it was probably not the best idea in the world.
2. You will be amazed at the lengths God will go to find you.
3. It wasn't about the honky-tonks and alcohol. It was about the singing.

Most evenings when I wasn't on the road, I walked to a small restaurant on the corner of my building. When the line is long and all the tables are full, the fastest place to eat when you're by yourself is at the bar. I popped in so often that the hostess remembered my name, and Fabiano Dos Santos, the sweet fella behind the bar, would pull out the place setting when he saw me coming. Then in his beautiful

Brazilian accent he would say, "Your usual peach tea, Momma? And fried chicken with turnip greens, right?"

Fabiano had served in the U.S. Army, become a citizen, and loved everything about America and country music. He became a Christian as a young teenager at a youth gathering in Brazil, and he provided a warm and welcomed smile during one of the most tumultuous times of my life.

One day, I fell apart on the stool, which is even worse than the stool falling apart on me. My mother had passed away a few days before. David was struggling and was away in a detox facility. Zach was at school in California, and Chera, well, she was still far away physically and emotionally. I had just about all I could take. Fabiano came around from behind the bar, hugged me super tight, and said, "You know what you need? You need a distraction. After work, come with me down the street." I know that sounds like either #MeToo or a proposition, but it was neither. We walked down the street to Printers Alley into Miss Kelli's Karaoke Bar.

That place became my *Cheers*. I'd go there every evening I was in town, hang out with the regulars, sing karaoke, and take my mind off everything that had gone wrong in my life. I know, I know, I grew up in a world where one is not supposed to hang out in a bar, but at that time in my life, it became a haven for me. At a time when everyone was giving me clichés and pat answers and telling me to pray more, a late-night group of crooners, waiters, and bartenders became my tribe. And boy, was I going to need them in the coming months.

Looking back, YES, there are probably much healthier places to hang out when your personal life is falling apart. I'm not recommending this path to anyone. A karaoke bar at 2:00 a.m. in a dark alley in Nashville, Tennessee, isn't exactly the right place to find spiritual guidance and sound advice. But for me at that moment, as crazy as it sounds, I found some of the kindest people, and frankly, it was just fun. Downright hilarious fun. At least, until it wasn't.

I had been dishing out fun for thousands of people in the world, but I rarely took time to have any fun myself. I'm not on a bowling team or in a sewing club. My small Bible study gals had dispersed years earlier. I had moved away from my small group at church, and truthfully, those gatherings held tough memories. Frankly, I rarely heard from anyone in those groups.

My rebellious middle-child heart reared her ugly head, I wanted to be someplace where very few people knew me, and if they did, they didn't care. Sadly, too often in my past, I found more comfort hanging out in a room full of sinners than with a congregation of saints who forgot they were once sinners. (Ouch, did I say that out loud? Ha!)

I have no idea who came up with the idea of karaoke. The word originated in Japan in the '80s. I'm pretty sure a bunch of Japanese folks sat around with a bottle of sake while Whitney Houston hit the high notes on the radio. They probably looked at each other and declared, "I bet I can do that!" Then they challenged each other, "No! No, you can't!"

I watched folks get up and absolutely butcher some of the greatest ballads of all time but do it with such conviction that, for a minute, I thought it really must be Lionel Richie, and they need to stop serving him alcohol!

Fabiano was right about one thing. It was a great distraction. Until it wasn't.

But if you're keeping a list like I used to do often with God:

Completely dysfunctional childhood. Check.
Loss of boundaries from sexual abuse. Check.
Sisters dead. Check.

Overworked and broken finances. Check.
Children gone. Check
Checked-out husband. Check.

There is something dangerous about trying to lose your troubles and yourself in the wrong places. I'm not just talking about hangovers and regrets. I got a few of those. Sorry to disappoint. Maybe I was trying to get back at David. He seemed to have found something that helped him wipe out misery while we were miserable. We were completely stunned by the choice our daughter made to leave us out of her life and the life of our grandson. It put a strain on just about every relationship that we shared with her. About five years into the whole ordeal, we got an email that she had had another a baby, another boy. David and I could barely speak her name. We floated around, shocked and broken, and the very thread that held our marriage and our life together was becoming thinner and thinner. Dramatic, I know. But if they ever do a movie of my life, that dark period in my past, well, I don't think there is any writing or acting that can depict the utter devastation of those days. How did I survive that? Sometimes, I really don't know. Wait! YES, I know how!

## CHAPTER 13

# JUST ONE THING

Folks often ask me, "How did you endure so much grief? How did you climb out of the dark?"

My scientific answer is, "Medicine balanced my serotonin, my hormones, my moods. Karaoke gave me a needed distraction, helped me laugh again. Gathering a new tribe of family and friends was imperative."

*All* these things were helpful or needed—except karaoke . . . it was just fun! But the *real* answer is the one thing. Just *one* thing.

One night a few years back, Andrew Tenenbaum called me and said he had a few extra tickets to the 25th Anniversary showing of *City Slickers*. I was ecstatic. Billy Crystal has always been a favorite of mine. Since Andrew was also his manager, chances were great that I would at least be in the same room. Not only was I in the same room, but Zach and I were seated directly behind him. Just before the movie started, a man slipped in late and sat right beside me. Of course, I began a little small talk. My enthusiasm and southern accent were just enough to annoy everyone around us so Billy would have to turn around. When he did, I was ready!

"Hi Billy, I'm Chonda. I'm a comic too. Andrew is my manager, so we're practically cousins!"

He smiled politely and shook my hand as Zach sunk down in his seat. I was on a roll! I turned to the man sitting beside me, "You must be family, a dear friend? You have a pretty good seat, so I'm guessing you might be Billy's tailor!" When I get nervous or feel out of place, my mouth often runs without a pinch of decorum or sophistication.

The gentleman looked sideways at me, and he may have rolled his eyes. "I'm Ron Underwood. I'm here for the Q and A afterward."

"Ah. Nice to meet you! And what did you do in the movie?"

"I directed it." Oops! I think in Hollywood it's supposedly a big deal to know these things!

Thank goodness the lights dimmed just as my face flushed bright pink and Zach whispered, "Mom, don't talk anymore!"

I love the movie *City Slickers*. Who doesn't? But the reason I bring it all up is this *one* thing. Do you remember the scene? Billy's character, Mitch, has been bouncing about on a horse for days with Jack Palance (Curly), a rugged cowboy who is tougher than nails and can rope a calf with his big toe. Mitch laments to Curly about his complicated midlife crisis. Curly finally asks, "Do you know what the secret to life is?" Mitch sits up taller on his horse. Leans in to hear. He's dying to know. Needs to know. It will be the glue that puts his entire life back together. Curly lifts his finger cradled in his dusty leather work glove, "It's this *one* thing. Just *one* thing."

Mitch says, "Your finger?"

"No!" Curly chuckles. "It's just *one* thing."

That's my answer, too. The secret to getting through anything starts with just *one* thing. Faith.

Has my faith ever wavered in strength? Yes, way too often. Have I questioned "why even bother?" You'd better believe it. Have I wondered if it works? Every other day. But you know what happens? The next day shows up. Then the next and the next. Before long, I've passed through one of the most difficult weeks of my life. Because of that *one* thing.

If you're expecting your faith to help you get something you want or fix everything, well, you might as well put your faith in a statue of a little fat man or buy a lottery ticket. There have been some tough days. Not as bad as the jump-in-the-river days. Days where I beg God, "Please, please fix this. Fix me. I can't make it through this anymore." Like the clink of a couple of coins into a slot machine, I pull the lever. Nothing.

Bart Millard is a songwriter and friend. I mean, it's not like I have his cell phone number and we toss around song ideas, but he must have some sort of spiritual connection with me because it never fails that when I am at a low point in my grief, missing David or the kids, a song he has written floats through my radio and speaks to me—like MercyMe's "Even If":

> I know You're able and I know You can
> Save through the fire with Your mighty hand
> But even if You don't,
> My hope is You alone[1]

Maybe faith is not about what you get. Maybe it's about who you become. Maybe it's not about believing your circumstances will change; maybe it's about believing in God even if they never do.

---

1 "Even If," MercyMe, Bart Millard, David Garcia, Ben Glover, Crystal Lewis, Tim Timmons, *Lifer*, Fair Trade Services, 2017.

Period. Not the getting. The giving of faith. The adoration regardless of the outcome. In that regard, I have never lost my faith. I have complete faith that God can change things, fix things. Sometimes He does, sometimes He doesn't. But putting my trust and faith in Him has changed me because I've learned what happens if I don't.

A better question might be, "Have you ever lost Chonda?" I'm pretty sure God would say, "Oh, a few times we came close. She tried to hide. She slipped to the shadows. Tried to jump in the river, but it was too shallow. I drained it on purpose. But I knew where she was the whole time."

Okay, what religion am I? What denomination do I align with? I'm a Protestant who at one point was mesmerized by the rituals of the Catholic Church. It all started when I went to Rome and decided I would make a great nun—other than the vows of chastity and obedience. Because nuns have boundaries along with their great rituals. I thought becoming one could help me get some. Later, I went to Israel and decided I wanted to be Jewish. The Jewish people have such great family traditions, and for someone starved for family connections, it seemed perfect. So, if there were some way to be part Protestant, Catholic, and Jewish, I would have signed up. Maybe I am Prostaholictish.

The actual church that has always felt like a *home church* is World Outreach in Murfreesboro, Tennessee; it's interdenominational and it's where I grew up spiritually. It was there that I learned what grace is supposed to look like. The Bible teaching there instilled in me a hunger for the Word of God. How I ended up there is an interesting story. I had been invited to perform at a large church in Fort Wayne, Indiana, where they speak in tongues. After doing some comedy, I sang a song that my big sister Charlotta had sung at church three days before she died:

"For whatever it takes, to draw closer to you, Lord . . ." and it moved people so much that they came forward and began passing out. I am 100 percent in favor of being moved by the Spirit but 100 percent against passing out in a dress because that means people can see more than they did even when I was crawling into the back of my Chevette in a skirt. I didn't understand a lot of it, but I did decide it may not be the church for me.

Sometime later, I was invited to speak to four hundred women at another church, again in Indiana. They put me in the parsonage cabin. That afternoon, I sat in the cabin reading my Bible. I started to feel sleepy, so I closed my eyes to take a catnap. When I woke up, the cabin was totally dark and gloomy. I panicked, thinking I had overslept and missed speaking, but the clock indicated it was only 3:00 in the afternoon. As I inhaled a deep breath of relief, I smelled something putrid. I looked everywhere thinking maybe there was a dead mouse or rat somewhere behind the refrigerator or under the couch. While searching for the source of the smell, I felt something brush past me. The hair on my arms and the back of my neck stood up. I tried to talk to whatever it was, but there was no answer. Fear gripped me and I began sweating. It felt and smelled like pure evil in that room. I ran over to my Bible laying on the couch and dropped to my knees and asked the Lord for help and protection. I started quoting every verse I knew to give myself courage. In a few moments, I opened my eyes. Everything calmed down and the smell of lilac and lavender filled the room as it brightened with daylight again.

Something had happened to me. I felt stronger. I felt empowered, and that night in the concert, I spoke with a deeper conviction and resolve to draw women to make a commitment to Jesus Christ. As odd as it may sound to you, all I know is that when I prayed, words would fill my mouth, tears would pour from my eyes, and I went home wanting to deepen my connection with God.

Back in Tennessee, I told my Nazarene pastor about my weekend. He said I had been filled with the Holy Spirit. As we talked, he said he felt I needed a church that could nurture this deeper connection I had found with God. He recommended I go to World Outreach Church in Murfreesboro. And that's how I ended up there. I wonder if that Nazarene pastor ever thought that my tithe was going to get a little better?

My faith is the power that helps me deal with my pain. It helps me realize that a lot of the pain I'm working through now is my own doing. That is called sweet conviction, and from a loving God, it is a good thing. For many years, I carried great guilt and took the blame for just about everything. Before you throw the Bible at me, I know that David's death was not my fault. I didn't hold him down and pour alcohol down his throat. But being too driven and absent too often, that's on me. Breaking his heart? I own that and hate it. And I must also own that some of my actions probably pushed the "elephant in the room" completely out of the zoo.

In other words, I am not saying that every terrible thing that has happened to you is all your fault either. That's not where I'm going at all. But there are consequences to our actions. An extra-large pizza with a side of breadsticks may soothe my troubled soul, but I will have to live with the thirty pounds on my hips for many years to come. I'm learning what I should be responsible for. Too much blame will lead to a heap of shame—let it go. Don't let your remorse be your ruin.

I have learned to lighten up on myself. I still beat myself for missing the warning signs, those *neon* signs from God that flashed before my eyes from time to time. But now I work at keeping my mistakes and trials in perspective. Just as God is alive and active in our lives, you must also beware that Satan is just as busy and active trying to bring you down.

One more unexplainable moment from God was in November 1996. David and I went to Focus on the Family in Colorado Springs. While we were excited about what was happening in my career, we noticed my material and stories about growing up as a preacher's kid resonated with a lot of preachers' kids that had forgotten how to chuckle about their past. The letters came every week, and David and I decided it would be wonderful to meet with several staff people to discuss what we could do to organize a support chain for adult preachers' kids. Throughout the day, people kept saying, "Hey before you leave, you should stop and pray with Dr. Gatewood." We had never met Dr. David Gatewood, but he was the head of the counseling department at that time. So before we left the building, we found ourselves sitting in his office. He was gentle, kind, and brilliant. He knew very little about me and David. He knew nothing of our background or dreams, which is what makes this story so amazing.

Christians and counselors, friends and fans, often ask, "Can I pray for you?" But Dr. Gatewood was different. He asked, "May I listen for you?" And that's just what he did—"listening prayer." This was a new one for me. Basically, it's where someone starts to pray, stops, and waits to hear from God. I'm a believer, but I was not sure how this was going to end up . . . and remember, I'm a believer with a comedian's viewpoint about everything. So, when he took a long pause in the middle of praying, I squeezed David's hand so I wouldn't start giggling. Suddenly, a chill ran down my spine. I looked around to see if God himself had walked into the room, because the timbre of Dr. Gatewood's voice had changed so much. As he began to speak, his wife grabbed a pad and pencil and wrote down every word.

Here is what he said:

*My special rhinestone cowgirl. Have I not given you the Spirit of clowning? My clowns are filled with tears. But your laughter without tears would not be laughter at all.*

*My zealous zestful daughter, enough of Arminian strongholds. Enough of the daggers of law.*

*I have called you to joy and peace and serenity. With me there is no striving. Hear this my daughter: your call is to walk in the wake of my striving. I have striven for you already. These are the mysteries of my Spirit. Ponder them and I will show you the way. Be a Mary—not a Martha. This one thing is needful.*

*I would hug you, my daughter. Come to me for your daily hug. I am not like your father. I am meek and humble in Spirit, and you will find rest for your soul. Teach my people, my wide-eyed wonder. Little-girl sparkles and childlike laughter. Minnie Pearl vision and Minnie Pearl games. I have not left you alone even now as we speak.*

*Your sensitive lover, David, was prepared before you were born. Silent lips, deep waters. Have you not given him your doleful tears? Bambi's mother shuddering, has he not been your stately stag?*

(To David) *Enough of silence, my son! Enough of writing secondhand. I will enhance your skills of writing through the prisms of your pain. You are different in your internal wounds. Alcohol drowning, hiding empty wounds. Speak forth your heart, my son. I will do the healing. You are not that different than the wife of your youth. Similar wounds, similar games. Speak to each other. Speak, my son, speak!*

*A threefold coil between you will become a threefold fused coil of steel which will carry the beacon of my light. You together will break three generations of silence. Fresh wind blowing for ten generations to come. This is my promise.*

*This is your destiny: light instead of darkness. Rainbows instead of trauma. Joy instead of mourning. Riches and fame instead of poverty.*

*Enough of the daggers of criticism and the swords of law. I have called you to mercy and not sacrifice. Enough of Arminian perfectionism and hypocrisies. My kingdom is wide and deeper than you know.*

*Be loyal to my family, a bigger family than you know. Loyalty to my Kingdom cannot be disloyalty to your heritage. Rhinestone cowgirl! Rhinestone preacher's kid.*

*You will play a tune. You will lead a dance to my millions of special kids. They will dance with you. You will charm them with my Spirit. Be a Mary, not a Martha. I will do this work. This is my work, not yours.*

*Come to my rock, sit in my shelter—bask in my warmth as David did in Psalms 61 and 62. Enough of the terrors of the night. Enough of the flying darts of the evil one. Enough of the fowlers snare among the people. Come sit under pinions and I will be your shelter, as the prophet David has said in Psalm 91.*

*Bright lights! Bright spotlights! You will see your name in greater lights if you honor me. I will honor you to a broken and hurt generation. Remember this is my work, my daughter. Be a Mary, not a Martha.*

I believe God gives us signals like listening prayer and neon signs to get us thinking. It's up to us to not miss them.

Right after we met with Dr. Gatewood, my career began to soar. David published his first book, his autobiography *Salvage*. You would think we were on our way. After all, the Bible says,

> So Christ himself gave the apostles, the prophets, the evangelists, the pastors and teachers, to equip his people for works of service, so that the body of Christ may be built up until we all reach unity in the faith and in the knowledge of the Son of God and become mature, attaining to the whole measure of the fullness of Christ.
>
> Then we will no longer be infants, tossed back and forth by the waves, and blown here and there by every wind of teaching and by the cunning and craftiness of people in their deceitful scheming. Instead, speaking the truth in love, we will grow to become in every respect the mature body of him who is the head, that is, Christ. From him the whole body, joined and held together by every supporting ligament, grows and builds itself up in love, as each part does its work. (Ephesians 4:11–16)

Unfortunately, that's when we really could have used the remote control, the do-over, the rewind, because life isn't a dress rehearsal unless you're Shirley MacLaine. No, you can't do it over. But you can learn from all of it.

That passage in Ephesians is the best explanation I can find for why David and I lived this roller-coaster life. We stayed in spiritual infancy far too often, far too long. And both growing up and not growing up have consequences.

## CHAPTER 14

# IF I HAD KNOWN THEN

In our youth, David and I weren't just two people getting married and starting a life together. We were two kids with broken backgrounds and a myriad of sights and scenes that shaped who we were. In other words, our one-plus-one equaled about a trillion! If only those were dollars we inherited from pristine, family-run, multimillion-dollar corporations.

As author BJ Neblett wrote, "We are the sum total of our experiences. Those experiences—be they positive or negative—make us the person we are, at any given point in our lives. And, like a flowing river, those same experiences, and those yet to come, continue to influence and reshape the person we are, and the person we become. None of us are the same as we were yesterday, nor will be tomorrow."[1]

It has been almost ten years since David died. I carry the grief pretty well *most days*. When the tears well up in my eyes and spill

---

1 BJ Neblett, "George (Part One)," *BJ Neblett* blog, July 2009, https://bjneblett.blogspot.com/2013/02/george-part-one.html.

over, most often it is not about wanting him here. I wouldn't want him here if he still had to carry the same pain and heartaches. Although I do wish he could see Zach learning to drive the tractor and taking care of the farm like he used to. No, my grief now is about wishing I could have a do-over.

"If only I had known then what I know now." Yes, it's cliché and trite, but read the words slowly and deliberately so you might learn something from our—and your—mistakes.

At one point, I realized I should have given David more of what he needed, and I am not talking about the Sunday roast. I validated his efforts often and tried to give him the freedom to show his skills and grow his skills as a writer. That worked for a while, but then his own past, his guilt, or his feelings of inadequacy would slither in like a cottonmouth snake in a Tennessee river. Try as I might, I couldn't fix us both. Good Lord, I had my hands full trying to fix me!

I think couples today should be required to spend more hours talking through their past and learning better communication skills than spending those hours registering for china or choosing the perfect caterer for their weddings. Each person doesn't simply become totally new when they walk down the aisle. They are two people carrying the same sets of wounds and dysfunctions after the ceremony. If you're lucky, your wounds and dysfunctions might complement each other. When David felt nervous, he got quiet and worked to be invisible. When I was nervous, I talked a mile a minute and refused to melt into the background. Perfect couple!

Near the last days of David's life, his drinking got worse, and his health began to fall apart, but I didn't realize how serious it was as I was finishing up a long tour.

Touring sounds fun—a fancy bus full of joyful friends watching late-night movies and doing Bible studies every afternoon. I'm laughing at the fond memories as I write this!

The crew stays busy most of the time. When the concert is over, they reconnect with their families and drag themselves off to bed because the next city may bring new challenges; then we start all over again. When we wind down a long tour, I take the crew out for dinner or invite their families to come over for a cookout—something to rinse the road dust off and get back into normal living.

This time, my assistant Cynthia had received an email from a travel company touting cheap trips to a spa in Mexico. That sounded great to me. Blue water, warm beach, a massage before tackling what awaited me at home. Ahhh, it sounded great. So, off we went: Cynthia, me, and a couple of girlfriends. It was so nice. And so needed.

David was hospitalized the day I returned from that little jaunt. We shared two moments in the hospital that I'll never forget. The first was when a nurse was asking him questions to check his level of alertness. "If I drop a rock in water, will it float or sink?" she asked.

"Depends on what water," David replied.

The nurse turned to me and shook her head sympathetically. "That's not a good sign. There could be some brain damage."

I grinned and patted David's hand. "Tell her what body of water you're thinking of, Honey." He sat up straighter and said, "The Dead Sea. Everything floats in the Dead Sea. I floated in the Dead Sea with a pile of rocks on my stomach."

The second moment was late one evening. About four or five days later, the doctors revived him from a medically induced coma. They knew he had a brain bleed, and they needed to see how much brain damage had occurred. The ICU itself is often a busy place. There are bells and whistles, gadgets and monitors galore. And with friends and family popping in, the medical staff in and out constantly, I felt like I was in a battle to have some alone time with David. But at night—that was our time. I had scooted my chair as close to him as possible, virtually daring someone to tell me to leave. God was merciful, and we had some truly meaningful and tender conversations. David knew he was in rough shape. I didn't want to talk about it. I wanted to pretend that all the wires and tubes would go away and soon we would be holding hands and walking the trails at the farm. I just wanted to tell him that I loved him and how sorry I was for any times I had hurt him. I felt ashamed for having been away on the road so much and for not realizing the treasure I had in him. I stroked his arm, wiped his face, and vowed we would make it through this and never let anything come between us again.

David lifted my hand to his lips, kissed it, then said, "I have been a really bad husband for a very long time."

"What? No. No, never," I said immediately.

"We never did know what we were doing," he continued, and in David Pierce fashion he added, "We just winged it!"

It would be months and years later before I realized how tender those words were for me. Shame will convince you that everything ugly, everything wrong in your life, is all your fault. I carried that guilt for way too long. I didn't want him to feel anything but encouragement to live. In a very small and subtle way, he gave me permission to own only my mistakes and leave the rest alone. I loved him more that day than ever before, and there is no doubt in my mind that he loved me as well.

Yes, we had some deep underlying problems in our relationship. In our thirty-one years of marriage—that's 11,315 days or 271,560 hours—about 2 percent weren't all that great. I've done the math and those are pretty good odds. I would live those days all over again.

Sadly, the worst of the 2 percent came too late to unravel. There was no time to fix anything, not even his tired and weary body.

On David's last day of life, I had stepped out to grab coffee. I walked in just as David winced and said he had pounding headache.

Just then, every gadget and monitor sounded off. The neurologist rushed in and began to shine a light into his eyes,

The nurse asked him, "Mr. Pierce, do you know who that is beside you?"

David replied, "Yes. It had better still be my wife!" Whew! I loved that man.

After emergency brain surgery to stop the bleeding in his brain, David never breathed on his own again. He was never conscious again. Being there for David's last breath was hard. We had taken him off life support. The doctor said it could take four minutes or it could take four hours. I hoped for that one surprising moment where David would sit up and say, "Oh, I'm better now. Let's go home." Everyone hopes that will happen when they unplug the machine.

I sang his favorite praise song to him as I held his hand, "Over the mountains and the sea, your river runs with love for me . . ."[2] David loved to climb mountains. At one point, he gripped my hand and squeezed hard. My eyes must have lit up as I glanced at the doctor. But he solemnly said it was an involuntary motion and David would soon take his last breath. And sure enough, he made one last heave and then his chest relaxed. I leaned forward and said, "Oh, Honey, are you leaving?" The room got quiet. "Oh, my Love, you are gone."

When I look back at our life and think of us together, I smile. David was my dearest friend. We had twenty-nine really great years in our thirty-one years together. Some people may think that's sad. Me? I think it's wonderful. If you're about to be married and you think nine out of every ten years are going to be great, sign up for

2 "I Could Sing of Your Love Forever," Delirious?, Martin Smith, *Cutting Edge 2*, Furious? Records, 1994.

that. Heck, two out of every three years is pretty awesome. It's worth it, because there is no such thing as a perfect marriage or perfect love between two fallible humans.

In the days and weeks to follow, Zach and I spent many days taking long walks at the Farm. We ordered David's headstone. We sat in his woodshop and tried to guess what in the world some of those tools were for. We cried plenty of tears and watched a few home movies. But mainly, we just kept breathing. My heart ached for Zachary. I saw something very familiar in him. What was it? Oh, yeah—*me!* My family unit drifted away in spurts of grief and pain, death, and dysfunction within a few years. The foundation I thought I knew had crumbled. And there was Zach, dealing with much of the same anger and pain; no contact with his sister, away from the town he grew up in, apart from friends who dispersed in college or the military, and now his father was gone.

It's one thing to carry your grief and pain, hurt and anger, but to watch your child carrying all those things as well. Whew. It was just about my undoing.

Before David got sick, I was in the middle of making a documentary. What started out as a "behind the scenes" piece about a semi-successful comic that Hollywood doesn't know became a poignant documentary of walking through great pain and still finding a way to laugh. We had sweet interviews with David. He was honest and open about getting sober. We had reconciled so many things, but our lives were still far from perfect.

The documentary came out after David died. As I watched it, I felt determined not to let our family drama stifle Zach's dreams or desires. I slapped on a smile and told him one morning, "You need to go back to California. Go back to what you were doing. I will be fine, and I am not your responsibility." So we began to sort through some of David's things so Zach could choose what he wanted to take to California. David's favorite Atlanta Braves shirt, favorite ball caps, his iPad, watch, shaving kit.

As we pulled in under the awning at the airport, Zachary sat very quiet for a moment. He took a deep breath and said, "Mom, I found something on Dad's computer and printed it off for you." He handed me the sheet of paper. It was a note to our first grandchild, Sawyer.

> *For Sawyer*
>
> *I want to show you living things in the woods and things I find under rocks and dead logs and teach you which ones are okay to poke and which to stay away from (and I will re-read the manuals before I do so, just to be sure).*
>
> *I want to show you the night sky and how to find the North Star and Betelgeuse (so easy once you know where it is). I want to point out where the heck Cassiopeia is—since there's a really great story that goes with that one.*
>
> *I want to teach you how to tie the three knots that I know—and, as far as I know, I only use them to teach others how to tie them. Although the blood knot is a cool one and has nothing to do with blood or vampires. And the double-whip finish is good for tying on fishing hooks.*
>
> *I want to teach you to fish and not just how to catch a fish. I want to teach you how to think like a fish.*
>
> *I want to teach you that there is a perfect golf swing. But you'll have to find that swing yourself, since I'm unsure of it—but I want to give you hope and encouragement that it does exist.*

*I want to give you a tool, like a hammer or a screwdriver, and an old kitchen appliance so you can take it apart. "Just whack it!" I'll tell you.*

*I want to build another tree house, this one with a better periscope. (Toys-R-Us has been improving their periscopes in the last sixteen years.) This one will have more secret compartments and trap doors and a kick-butt communications system.*

*I want to go to your third-grade class and lecture on the winter solstice because you've told everyone I'm an expert about winter solstice.*

*Then at some point—not too late into life—I hope to die before you figure out I'm just an average, scared man who has tried all his life to figure things out as he goes.*

*To esteem the former is easy. And the former should be celebrated wildly. To understand the latter requires love that transcends all warts. A love that may last forever but can only be voiced for a short while.*

*Is that too much to expect? Because I have more paper.*

I sobbed.

If there is any story or picture that I could use to illustrate to you exactly who my husband was and what he was like—it is this note. It is his sense of humor, his brilliance, and his beautiful heart. He was utterly brokenhearted when he typed out those words and yet he managed to make you smile and chuckle reading it.

As I wiped my face, all I could say to Zach was, "Zach, your dad is not in pain anymore. Where he is now, Zach, he is hiking and fishing and waiting on the porch for us. You cannot miss heaven, Zach."

Zach smiled, then his face grew stern, "Mom, there is something else. I have Dad's phone. I'm going to leave it with you. And one night when you feel strong, I want you to read through his text messages. Because you need to know . . . someone you might think is your friend. Well, they're not."

I told him I would look at it later. "Zach, I'm going to be fine. The best thing you can do for me and your dad is stay strong and smart and love Jesus."

When I got back home, I took a deep breath and plugged in David's phone. I read some kind and sweet texts from family. Work-related messages. Fun banter between David and Zach. Long messages between David and me. Some sweet, some resounding with desperation. "Where are you?" "Are you headed home from the Farm?" "Did you eat something?" "Please, David. Please don't drink today."

I read through everything. It reminded me of the life we shared. It felt like David had just been in the room five seconds ago, and in an instant, he vanished.

Then I came across the messages Zach warned me about—someone I had confided in, and within her texts to David, she had scrolled out every secret I had ever shared with her. Zach was right. She was not a friend at all. My heart sank.

When I started this book, I wrote pages about this. I filled my manuscript with how it feels to be disappointed in people you thought you could trust. Character flaws I saw years earlier. A long diatribe about manipulation. But I stopped. This story is not about what's wrong with other people. Besides, in some nutty way, I miss her. We shared years of life together, but I cannot afford to bring her back into my life ever again.

Reading through the text thread, I realized I had ignored some warning signs. Maybe I didn't want to believe what my heart was trying to reveal. I must let her go because I put way too much power in her hands—too much power over me. That's why it felt like a giant betrayal. One thing I have learned is that letting go doesn't mean you don't care. It just means the only thing I can fix, change, or control is ME.

Often when I am overly concerned about something someone said or did and the chatterbox in my brain rears its ugly head, Zach gets an earful about it at the dinner table. He will put his hand on my arm and say, "Mom. Mom, don't let them get in your head." Easier said than done sometimes. That's why I keep my counselor and my pastor on speed dial.

I can always tell when true emotional healing has taken place in my life. For me, it is most often accompanied with great peace. And sometimes that healing swoops in and takes your breath away like a flowing river. My friend and fellow comedian Marlo Rutz wrote a book called *God Sprinkles*. She defines a God Sprinkle as, "God's providence and the supernatural of God revealed in the natural of every day."[3]

Talk about a sprinkle—flash forward about five years from the day David died. I had a flood.

My assistant, Glynda, and I were giving the cabin at the Funny Farm a little facelift one day. That means a few new throw pillows, candles, and lamps. Everyone who knows Glynda Maxey knows the first step in decorating any room or sprucing up any house is pillows and lamps! I've counted twenty-four pillows on her bed in my guest bedroom and snapped a photo so I would know exactly the order they should go in when I make the bed.

As we rearranged a few things, I got sidetracked—as usual. *"Squirrel!"* I began to lament to her for the fiftieth time about how I longed to find David's wedding ring. After David was buried, I found his original ring in an old jewelry box at home. It was thin and had

3 Marlo Rutz, *God Sprinkles* (Laughter, Light and Love Publishing, 2021), 26.

cost all of $102 in 1983. The jeweler had to cut it to widen it for his finger. But that was not the ring he wore every day. While on a trip to Israel for our fifteenth wedding anniversary, we upgraded. He bought me a much larger diamond, and I bought him a new wedding band inscribed inside with "David, my Beloved" in Hebrew. He loved it, and I can't remember him ever taking it off.

But somewhere between rehab facilities and hospital stays . . . it vanished. In my head I had written the script out. *That ring is probably at the bottom of the lake at the farm.* I felt certain he had been so angry at me one day for cutting him off from extra money for alcohol. I bet he was put out with me for making him stay in rehab. I had no doubt he had some raging moment when I told him we needed to separate financially because if he killed someone drinking and driving, we could lose everything. I bet that once-trusted friend insinuated one time too many, "Are you sure Chonda is traveling alone this weekend?" and in a jealous rage he threw that ring out the window. I prayed about a million times that God would help me find it. I searched for it for three years at the farm. The workshop, the cabin, his fishing tackle box, his golf clubs. And all the while, what I had written in my head was haunting and sad.

As I dusted the desk that day, I accidentally knocked over a little wooden index box that was filled with BBs for an old BB gun. BBs spilled out and bounced and rolled into every crack of the pine floor. Glynda came running with the broom and dustpan, and I started sweeping. I don't know if the ring was already there or if those little copper beads simply led me to a bigger shimmer under the desk. But there it was. I dropped to the floor and began to sob. I clutched that ring like Frodo in *The Lord of the Rings*. At that moment, it became my dearest treasure. Then, amid the thousands of BBs, I also found a crumpled piece of paper in David's handwriting. A recipe for peanut butter cookies! David loved any recipe that had peanut butter in it. It simply made me smile.

As I stood up, still clutching the ring to my heart, I realized the story in my head had been wrong. The script flipped almost immediately. David didn't throw his ring in the lake. He probably put it in the box because it was getting tight. He could have taken it off when he was staining the desk. I won't know until Heaven, but what the devil had tried to convince me for months to discourage me was a lie. I let the devil "get in my head." Nothing I had imagined was true.

An old hymn rang in my ears . . .

> Peace, peace, wonderful peace,
> Coming down from the Father above,
> Sweep over my Spirit forever, I pray,
> In fathomless billows of love.[4]

At that moment, my tears were not sobs of sadness. They were delightful, happy tears. I knew the truth in my heart, in my spirit. I was at peace.

---

4 "Wonderful Peace," Warren D. Cornell, public domain, 1892.

## CHAPTER 15

# THERE IS NO GLORY IN THIS STORY

***Note:*** *My therapist and counselor extraordinaire, Tracey Robinson at Branches, explained to me that there are four basic ways that our bodies deal with the onset of fear and trauma. The Four principles are these: Fight, Flight, Flee, or Fawn. It is why some will run at the first sight of trouble while others simply freeze in place. Many will lash out, fight it out . . . while others become Chatty Cathy or the hostess-with-the-mostest trying to defuse or deflect the situation hurtling their way. I'll let you guess which one of those descriptions fits yours truly!*

***This chapter is difficult and may be a trigger for those who have experienced sexual assault. If this brings up any uncomfortable feelings in you—please stop reading and contact a counselor or your support group.***

I started to work again about two years after my husband died. The road felt like an old friend. I had missed the faces in crowds and the sound of their laughter. The pace was doable, and frankly, a mortgage waits for no one! After the shows, I would step out and sign books. The interaction was like a healing balm. Widows came in all shapes and sizes, ages, and stages. A documentary about my life, *Laughing in the Dark*, had struck a chord, and the sincere outpouring of love touched me deeply. However, standing for hours signing books and CDs for hundreds of women almost became like standing by the casket at the funeral home. After a while, it was too much emotionally, so my tour manager at the time laid a spiral notebook out each night so folks could write their messages. I cherish them to this day.

Even though I love being on a stage, I felt like it was a battle to get some alone time. Though I make people laugh for a living, I often must force myself to go anywhere socially, especially since David died. But one evening in 2016, I went out for dinner with some friends. At that time, loneliness was so horrific in my life. Have you ever been so lonely that a little conversation with the postman, the trash collector—anyone—was the highlight of your day? Heck, I've had conversations with squirrels running across the road because I craved companionship. Maybe that skewed my judgment at the time. Nevertheless, I didn't see a signal light, a warning sign that countless smarter women have learned. The thought of a strange man outside the building who may have followed me home after that dinner never entered my mind. I hadn't been a single woman out and about in more than forty years.

When I went home, he entered my apartment building as if he were a friendly neighbor. I got on the elevator by myself. Later, the security cameras would show that he went the opposite way—until the elevator door closed. Then he looped back around and watched the floor numbers. And then he stepped onto the next elevator that took him to my floor. I walked into my condo, threw my purse on the counter, and went to my room. I started to get ready for bed when I heard something in the living room. I threw on a robe, and as I stepped into the living room, I was startled to see him standing beside my piano. I have no idea if he walked in right behind me, if I had forgotten to lock the door, or if he jimmied the lock. Regardless, he was in my apartment.

He said he just wanted to make sure I got in and began to walk closer. I'll spare you the rest of the details, but suffice it to say, he raped me. It was ugly and it was violent. It was *nothing* like sex between two people who love each other.

I went through the whole nine yards with the police. Endured the rape kit ordeal. Cried. Called my counselor. Cried some more. Days later, I made a tough decision. I dropped it. I didn't pursue criminal charges against the guy. I chose to endure the shame in private because I was afraid. I wanted nothing to come out in the paper, and I never wanted to sit on the witness stand in a courtroom. It wasn't the usual shame that accompanies these horrific moments for women. Nope. I was afraid...of you. I was afraid of what my fans would think of me.

As many women do after such a trauma, I felt ashamed and dirty. I've since learned, of course, that being raped is not a woman's fault. Sure, we can all take precautions and keep our eyes open and radar up, but being forced into sex by someone bigger and stronger is not a choice. It's a crime. And none of us should define ourselves by what happened to us.

A few weeks later, my doctor suggested another exam, pap smear, etc. Surprisingly, this time she found a small tumor. It seems I have the gene marker that indicates I have a propensity for cervical cancer. For about six months, I told people I had the PBR marker, but then I found out that stands for Pabst Blue Ribbon, which I do not have a propensity for. Consequently, I had three tumors removed, and they were all benign. In a very strange and bizarre way, what happened to me had a positive benefit. I am not recommending it as a good way to have an early detection of cancer; it's just proof once again of the mysterious ways in which the Lord works. As the Apostle Paul wrote, "And we know that in all things God works for the good of those who love him, who have been called according to his purpose" (Romans 8:28).

I have a list of things I am horribly ashamed of. Most of them are tucked deep in the back of my mind. Many of them are faint memories, like a tiny scar barely noticeable after years of new growth, long chats with my counselor, and better choices and habits. I could have a Ph.D. in learning from my mistakes. And yes, I've made the same mistake twice to make sure I learned it. By going broke twice, I learned how to manage my money (or at least to stop being so gullible)—like don't loan people money that you need yourself or that you know you are going to need paid back. Because 99.9999 percent of the time, you will never see it again. Don't trust accountants who can't count, and don't trust managers who charge you 52 percent of your income. I like to see the good in people, but in show business, I have met some unscrupulous characters and lost a lot of money trusting them.

I have learned to hold people more accountable for what they are supposed to be doing for me. For example, when I do a show, the promoter is supposed to do exactly what his title is—promote me. A promoter accidentally sent me an email that was clearly not intended for me. In it, he said Chonda is selling out, so let's promote our other clients then lay the radio promotion cost onto her shows. *Whoops.*

Those things hurt. They cause you to lose trust—even in good people. I want to trust, but sometimes the people I've trusted and believed had my best interests at heart really didn't give one hoot about me. I also will never make the mistake again of spending money to make a DVD just to get on *The Ellen DeGeneres Show* or *The Tonight Show.* I am so past that...although, if their talent booker happens to be reading this, call me.

I just realized if I start listing all my mistakes, this is going to become a 1,200-page book. If the list of mistakes was *all* I let define me, this entire book would be a waste of time for everyone. My advice is for you to learn from the mistakes you've made and don't make them again.

Mustering up a tiny scoop of pride in your life is sometimes almost impossible until you learn to forgive yourself. I have had to forgive *me* more times than I can count. And believe me . . . *me* is sometimes more than I can handle alone. But with Jesus, I have never been alone. Never. Regardless of my own stupidity or sin, He has been relentless. No matter how shameful, He is shameless in his pursuit to love me, despite how little I love myself. And He never fails to send a sign, a person, a reminder.

I have a new songwriter friend, Ben Fuller. His song "Chasing Rebels" left me sitting on the couch in my living room in a heap. And that's not always a bad thing.

> I ain't one to hide my stupid and my stubborn
> I won't lie about the ally's where I've been
> I won't ever try to cover all the lies that pulled me under
> Nearly buried in a box of my own sin
> And this freedom that I've found is not a platform
> For me to boast in anything that I have done
> It's just a messy canvas, of God's mercy in my madness
> And a fiery love that I could not outrun

When it comes to failure, you're no different
When it comes to shame, you're not alone
From prodigals on barstools
To pretenders in the church pews
Nobody's ever really too far gone

I find no glory in my story
All the times I ran away
And I'm not proud of where I've been
And all the choices that I've made
But if my past is now your present
I'm prayin' you see how
There's an unrelenting, comin' for you Savior
Who loves chasing rebels down[1]

Believe me, a heap of sobbing tears can sometimes have a better cleansing effect than juicing up something green with vinegar gummies. (Yes, I've tried that too!) You can't linger there—but there have been times that I have sat on a bench at the cemetery and just had a good old-fashioned, snot-dripping, tear-streaming, sobfest. Afterwards, I walk back to the house and truly feel like I have lost about three pounds in body fluid. I should probably sob and walk a few miles afterwards to double my efforts!

There is something purging about pouring it all out. And purging isn't pretty. Trouble is, if the dam cracks just a little about one incident in my life—there will be an avalanche of grief and regret that will burst through and flood a perfectly nice day.

If that happens to you, wade through it. Dry yourself off and square your shoulders—there's an "unrelenting, coming-for-you Savior" who will wade through flood and fire to rescue you.

---

1 "Chasing Rebels," Tony Wood, Michael Farren, Ben Fuller, Curb Records Inc./ Essential Music Publishing LLC, 2022.

CHAPTER 16

# VALIDATION AND VULNERABILITY

I often laugh when someone says to me, "Thank you for being so transparent and vulnerable." I will chuckle and reply, "I'm not all that transparent—I'm just lonely and needed someone to talk to!" Honestly, I have said many times on stage and off, "Comedy saved my life!" The medicine in the sound of laughter is remarkable. But the medicine I receive in validation when I deliver in comedy has been a gift to me in my brokenness. There are few occupations in which you can receive instant gratification or instant rejection within minutes!

There is nothing scarier than standing in front of large crowd, delivering a few lines, and hearing dead silence. Not a sigh, a chuckle—nothing. That happened from time to time in my early days. But once you feel that long drop of sweat running all the way down your back and into your underwear, you quickly learn where and when to take your chances and how to recover fast when a joke bombs. Because that sinking feeling of bombing feels like standing butt-naked in front of a room full of supermodels!

If I may brag just a little, it's been a long time since I absolutely bombed. Believe me, I have had jokes that didn't land well (as the polite chuckle would indicate). But thankfully, I have never been booed or chased off the stage. Yes, it could be that most of my audiences are really nice people. However, in defense of me, a forty-dollar ticket is still forty dollars, and I had better be at least fifty dollars' worth of funny no matter how nice the audience is. People will quit coming if I fail to deliver.

After thirty years, they keep coming. And no one is more surprised than me! I found a connection with my audience early on, and I'm not sure the comedy had a lot to do with it. I think it's because I've never done what I do just for the laughs. Lucille Ball once said, "I'm not funny. What I am is brave!" I completely get that.

I think my true connection with my audience has a lot to do with my willingness to be vulnerable. Comedy as a trade inherently requires some measure of vulnerability, but I've always wanted to leave my audience with a bit of vulnerability about myself in something I've learned along the way. And most lessons I've learned have been through the messy times, the broken times, the grief.

Psychologist and author Brené Brown says in a TED Talk, "Vulnerability sounds like truth and feels like courage. Truth and courage aren't always comfortable, but they're never weakness."[1]

The bloviated stories of painting the visiting evangelist's cat, wearing three pairs of Spanx, or hiking my toe up to the sander in the garage for a pedicure . . . that's comedy. But the last half of every concert comes with a love for those who are kind enough to listen. Brené Brown also said in the TED Talk, "Vulnerability is the birthplace

1 Brené Brown, "The Power of Vulnerability," TEDx, June 2010, https://www.ted.com/talks/brene_brown_the_power_of_vulnerability?language=en.

of love, belonging, joy, courage, empathy and creativity. It is the source of hope, empathy, accountability and authenticity. If we want greater clarity in our purpose or deeper and more meaningful spiritual lives, vulnerability is the path."

For me, becoming vulnerable led to being validated. For years, that need for validation came up way too often in my life. Through working with some amazing counselors, I've learned where some of this insecurity comes from. No stable father? That's obvious. Religion? More specifically, legalism. Given that my first introduction to knowing God was about fulfilling a long list of rules and regulations, it seemed impossible to please Him. No validation there! Trying to gain God's approval only resulted in a constant feeling of never measuring up.

The courage to speak about the tough stuff has not been easy. For instance, many years ago, a local Tennessee newspaper published the usual "local girl makes good" article about how I had met Minnie Pearl and how my dad had abandoned my family when I was in my teens, leaving me to help support my mom and pay the bills. My dad's second ex-wife sent the article to wife #3, because hell hath no fury like a woman scorned who scorned an earlier woman, and the minute my dad saw the article, he decided to threaten to sue me for defamation. What smarter way for a dad to make up for all the pain he caused than to try and sue his offspring? He sent me a scathing letter that included a long list of people he threatened to send it to. Oddly enough, he sent a copy of a receipt for a dishwasher that he bought Mom ten years prior and a copy of a receipt for a pair of glasses that he paid for when I was sixteen. He sent a letter to my brother as well.

Soon after the newspaper article came out, I was featured on the cover of *Today's Christian Woman.* I was so excited. I was especially tickled for my mother. In that issue, I spoke honestly about dealing with my father's mood swings and praised my mom for her courage and strength. It was a truly significant moment in my career and personal life. Once again, my father hated it. This time he sent threatening letters to me and to the magazine. When his letter arrived, I was mortified. I called the editor at *Today's Christian Woman* in tears. I told her I was willing to take a polygraph; I could send her names of people who could corroborate my story. She was so kind. She said, "Chonda, we don't publish anything without checking into the stories." She went on to explain that they had checked into him months ago. "Let's just say, your father is still not a well man, and we stand by you 100 percent."

Back then it seemed, as I began to reveal more truth about my life, my brother was less and less enthused about revealing any of it. I sent him my very first manuscript titled, "Second Row, Piano Side." I told him he deserved to read it before it was published because it revealed parts of his life as well. But my brother was in a very different emotional place than I was back then. He rarely spoke of our childhood, and he was yet to start a journey of healing that would change his life forever. At the time, my greatest fear in the world was losing his love and approval. He told me then, "I'm not reading it, Chonda. Why should I? I don't have to read it. I lived it. And no one is going to believe us." Sigh.

Flash forward to 2006. After an amazing transformation and a willingness to be vulnerable, my brother wrote in his book *Failure and How I Achieved It*, "I doubt if most psychologists would state that addiction is entirely an acquired behavior. There is a genetic predisposition. There are personal choices. There are the twists and turns of fate, and somehow, even the providence of God. But it was on the training ground of my childhood home where I conceived the coping mechanism that gave birth to my addiction. In my home that coping mechanism was secrecy. Just don't talk about it. Refuse to admit there is a problem. And above all, never let the world around you know that anything is wrong."[2]

Talk about getting vulnerable. My brother lost everything, went to rehab, then watched God's miraculous mercy give him back everything and more. He was, is, and always will be my superhero.

Both of us looked for validation in different ways. Both of us have a story we now share. Both of us recognize the miraculous work of healing that comes from being vulnerable first and foremost with God. My brother felt a greater obligation to keep checking in on Dad. I think there is a father/son element that I can't possibly get. At the same time, there is a father/daughter element that perhaps leaves a much more fearful aspect. I had little to do with my father for the last twenty or more years. That doesn't mean I had no compassion. I sent money several times through my brother or nearby pastors when needed. Dad was always in my prayers, and I am eternally grateful for being born.

My brother called one day in 2017 to tell me our father was dying. Mike passed his phone number along to me in case I chose to call. I wrote it on a piece of paper and stared at it for a week. No one wants to open a can of emotional worms. That's probably why I will never watch the movie *The Notebook* again. Those wiggly emotions are hard to get back in the jar sometimes.

One morning a few days later, I woke up feeling strong. I wasn't afraid. I realized I had nothing to lose. Regardless of tears I would cry or words my dad might say, good or bad, my forgiveness toward him was complete. I had relinquished his ability to control or hurt me. I

2 Mike Courtney, *Failure and How I Achieved It: A Journey from Addictions to Hope* (Murfreesboro, Tennessee: Branches Recovery Center, 2006), 23.

picked up the phone and dialed the number. I thought maybe it would help his passing and bring him some peace that all was as it should be.

His wife answered. I said, "This is Chonda. I'd like to speak to my dad." She told me he had been a bit out of it, and he was on a morphine drip, but she knew he would be glad it was me. Soon I heard what I assumed was him breathing on the other end, so I said, "Dad, this is Chonda."

No response.

I tried again. "Dad? Are you there? I heard you're not feeling too well."

Finally, he said, "No I'm not doing too good at all. But I am so happy to hear your voice."

There was a long pause, as neither of us knew what to say after that. He may have paused to see if I would mention the unmentionable. I waited to see if he would try and make amends. There was no apology, no begging for forgiveness, no explanations at all, but I honestly didn't expect that. And more importantly, I didn't need it. That's because I forgave him. I had the power to forgive him, and it didn't matter if he accepted it. I was in charge and was strong enough to call, and without a word from me, he knew I forgave him simply because I called.

"Dad, I understand you may not be in this world much longer," I said. "But you and I both know the next world will be the best ever."

He gave a little chuckle and agreed, "Oh yes, yes. I'm ready, honey."

I told him to tell Charlotta and Cheralyn hello for me. I said Mom was there and David would be waiting on a bank somewhere with an extra fishing pole. "Ya'll go fishing and catch a few 'til I get there." And yes. I cried. But not long.

From the moment I hung up the phone, I felt so good inside, as though the peace that passes understanding had flooded my soul. There is tremendous freedom in forgiveness. My dad died the next day. I didn't go to his funeral. I didn't need to, and at long last, I no longer needed my dad to validate me.

We all need validation. I think it's part of the human need for connection. I can stand on a stage in front of thousands of people who are laughing, crying, and applauding. But I still struggle sometimes to receive validation from people I love. I've learned if you want to grease your way into a dark pit, look for validation from the wrong people.

Dr. Jill Bolte Taylor wrote the book *My Stroke of Insight: A Brain Scientist's Personal Journey*. In it, she says, "Just like children, emotions heal when they are heard and validated."[3] Isn't that crazy? I am blessed and grateful to have had a mother who loved me and was proud of me. And to know that she acknowledged my pain—that is a treasure. But if I continued to live my life longing for the validation of others, especially others who may not be capable of doing so, well, I might start checking the water levels in the river again.

It's been a long journey for me to crawl out of my hole of neediness and stand securely on my own two feet. My value and worth are already within me.

Mike also wrote in his book, "My failure is the greatest thing God has ever done for me. It wasn't until I really failed that I learned to be at peace, that I accepted His grace, and I knew I was loved. My failure, my very lowest point, was the place where God turned my eyes away from me and pointed me to all He had done for me and all that He would still do. I had to get flat on my back to finally look up and see the future He wanted me to have."[4]

---

3 Jill Bolte Taylor, *My Stroke of Insight: A Brain Scientist's Personal Journey* (New York: Penguin Books, 2009), 164.
4 Courtney, *Failure and How I Achieved It*, 158.

Your journey is unique. It may not look like your siblings'. You may not handle things in the same ways. You may not even have the same scars or wounds. But it is still your story. I am reminded of one last quote from Brené Brown: "There will be times when standing alone feels too hard, too scary and you'll doubt your ability to make your way through the uncertainty. Someone, somewhere will say, 'Don't do it, you don't have what it takes to survive the wilderness.' This is when you reach deep into your wild heart and remind yourself, 'I am the wilderness.'"[5]

Here's an even better quote: "That is why, for Christ's sake, I delight in weaknesses, in insults, in hardships, in persecutions, in difficulties. For when I am weak, then I am strong" (2 Corinthians 12:10).

The world needs to hear what has been poured into your heart and how valuable you are to God, and none of us will do it in exactly the same way.

When David and I were engaged, we registered at the local department store bridal registry. I didn't know anything about such things. Remember, I was the only girl left in my family to have a wedding, and I didn't exactly travel in high society social circles.

At the department store, the clerk walked me through the store, clipboard in hand, and asked me which pattern of china I liked most. I picked out Blue Chintz Noritake. Not too expensive, but not too cheap. Maybe not cheap enough. Because come wedding day, we received three dinner plates, a salad plate, two bowls, and one cup and saucer. A couple of moves and a toddler later, I had two chipped dinner plates, one cereal bowl, and a cup left.

5 Brené Brown, *Braving the Wilderness* (New York: Random House, 2017), 163.

By then, Chera came along and started using her favorite Sesame Street Big Bird plastic plate. If we had more than four people over for dinner, it was a BYOP (bring your own plate) event. Soon it got to where I had to stop and wash dishes in the middle of dinner or have people eat in shifts. My solution was to start collecting S&H Green Stamps from the supermarket. If you collected an entire book of stamps, you could cash them in at the Piggly Wiggly for an entire set of dishes. Well, at least four place settings. But then I learned that you can't put those Piggly Wiggly dishes in the dishwasher because it will wash all the flowers off.

On Sundays, Mother would come over for dinner with her sweet husband Sammy. I would set the table with two Noritake china plates, a Sesame Street Big Bird plate, and a couple of flowerless Piggly Wiggly plates, and by then we had to add in Zachary's Teenage Mutant Ninja Turtles plate as well. Hint: You can also reuse those fancy microwavable dinner plates if you don't nuke them too long.

As a result, my Sunday dinner table was an eclectic variety of chipped dishes for many years. Then one afternoon, while scraping leftover mashed potatoes off the china plate into the garbage disposal and rinsing leftover green beans off Zach's Ninja Turtles plate, it dawned on me. Mashed potatoes can be served on a fancy Blue Chintz Noritake plate the same way they can go on a Big Bird plate. In other words, it *never* mattered for one minute what the container was. It's all about what it contains.

I no longer look for validation "out there" to help me feel better about myself. I must find substance and gratification on the inside first. What I "contain" must be validation enough—no matter how chipped and flowerless, no matter how battered and broken. What is inside is what matters.

I love to quote that great and masterful theologian, Dr. Seuss. He says it brilliantly:

Today you are you, that is truer than true.
There is no one alive who is Youer than You.[6]

This Chonda container is not a piece of fine china. I am more like a Big Bird plastic platter. But the foundation of hope I have found in Jesus Christ and the healing He has directed in my life changed everything for me. My faith hasn't sheltered me from life's tough blows and my own stupidity, but it has proven to give me the confidence that I have needed to keep pushing forward, to survive, even when life throws me its worst.

6 Dr. Seuss, *Oh, The Places You'll Go!* (New York: Random House, 1990).

## CHAPTER 17

# THE ART OF WIDOWHOOD

David's death put me in a private club that I never dreamed I would join. This club gets new members way too often, and it existed long before I ever noticed or understood it. Growing up, I thought a widow was a little old lady at church. It seemed sad. I had great sympathy. But as I got older, I began to notice younger and younger widows. From military wives to those who lost a spouse from cancer or disease, widowhood is without a doubt one of the most difficult roads a married person may ever walk. It is hard but not impossible. As the Apostle Paul wrote, "We are hard pressed on every side, but not crushed; perplexed but not in despair; struck down but not destroyed" (2 Corinthians 4:8).

If you are newly widowed, my best advice is to keep breathing. Keep walking but allow yourself to grieve. Often, with great love comes great grief. Don't try to squelch it. Give yourself time.

I found that establishing new routines for myself was helpful. The challenge, of course, was to stick with them. I also signed up for an art class. My job kept me out often, so my paintings began to look more like Vincent van Gogh's than I had intended. I got a blue ribbon at the nursing home for "special recognition," which really means "take your painting home because we are sure a first grader helped you with your homework"!

The internet is filled with amazing DIY ideas. Maybe you always wanted to write. Writing and journaling is an amazing way to find some healing in your life. Scrapbook. Volunteer at church. In other words, keep moving. Think of something you've always wanted to try. Do something that is not wrapped around every memory with your husband. I loved fishing and golfing with David. I was no good at any of it. But I loved all of it. I was about four years into widowhood before I could pick up a fishing pole without shedding a few tears. But soon, I was able to enjoy it all again. Golfing is another story. It's been over nine years, and my clubs are still collecting dust. I loved golfing with David, but Nancy Lopez I will never be, and frankly, I don't really miss it.

Along the way, I've learned a little better how to be wary of stupid people. Believe me, they are out there. Some show up early. Like the lady who asked, "Have you thought about dating? I think you should get right back out there!" The question itself wasn't so bad, but she was standing in the funeral home with my dead husband about twenty feet away. Insert that eyeroll emoji here! Some people wanted to offer hope. They were well-meaning, no doubt. But if you ask me, it was more like false hope.

Here are some things I heard after David died.

"If you see a red cardinal on your fence, it means your late husband is thinking about you." Who makes this stuff up? I probably heard that line three hundred times. I'm pretty sure my husband would not be sitting on my porch banister pooping all morning!

Here's another one: "If you see a blue butterfly, and it lands on your left shoulder, it means your husband is in heaven wishing you were there." My husband wants me dead? I don't get that one.

Really, what happens if you see a red cardinal, and a blue butterfly lands on your shoulder, then the red cardinal eats the blue butterfly? What is that supposed to mean? My husband has come back as a bug-eating Peeping Tom?

Most women who say these things to you have no idea what it is like to be a widow. It's almost like they are jealous. Somebody should check in on *their* husbands—just in case they come up missing!

Now, as a widow myself, I want to be helpful with advice. But I am no expert. I was probably given over twenty-five books from friends about death and dying. Many were written by widows. *Those* books I read because I want to hear from someone who *really* knows.

My advice right now is not for widows, but for FOWs. Friends of widows. So, dear dear reader, if you know a widow, get out a notepad and copy this down. Then rip out the pages and put them in your purse. Take a picture so you can refer to them when needed.

Here is the most important thing I can tell you: Just be there. Listen to them. Talk only when necessary. Because what most widows need is time and a loving friend in the room.

Most widows simply need to learn how to breathe again. It may take six months, it may take six years, but eventually they learn to breathe, unless they have a big date and they're wearing three pairs of Spanx. But until they can breathe again, the best thing to do is to shut up and listen. By the way, guys, if you're married, that is also good advice for dealing with a wife. Just shut up and listen. If you do, you decrease the chance she will kill you and make herself a widow.

And here is my best tip for widows. It's okay to be angry at God. Seriously, He can take it. But don't dwell there. After you're done being mad at the Lord, thank Him for giving you all the good moments when your husband was here. I tried that and it helped.

Now, more than ten years in as part of the widow's club of survivors, I've decided I will never marry again. I have so many problems that would ruin my dating life. Like my bladder. Imagine I find a new man. Some new man I meet online is not gonna get the fact my bladder has a mind of its own. David got it. I hear water running, I pee. I laugh, I pee. I see a Culligan Water delivery truck, I pee. Although, I have a solution for women like me. Why don't they put Depends right into the Spanx? Once you squeeze them on, something squeezes out.

Rather than get married again, I've decided the best way to handle widowhood is to grieve in a way that honors David's life—by trying to be a good person and a good citizen and a good friend to people I know and to friends I have yet to meet. And guess what? It's working. Well, I say that, but catch me on a lonely night . . . it's another story.

For a starting point, I asked myself, what is the one thing all women need? The answer is a no-brainer. Girlfriends. I say on stage often, "Who is here with you? I hope you all have a tribe of gals you depend on. I also hope you have that one woman in your tribe that you talk about when you get together!" Yeah, we have that one too. We love her. But most of our conversations about her start with, "After she gets out on parole . . ."

Women need girlfriends like corn needs rain, like a scuba diver needs air, like Willie Nelson needs weed. Without true friends, we can't survive. I am blessed with great girlfriends even though I haven't always been one myself. At first, I didn't do the whole girlfriend thing very well, and I didn't need my therapist to tell me why. I figured it out all by myself. It started with moving around so much when I was little. My two sisters were the one constant in my life, the two friends that I knew would be there for me and with me when we moved from town to town. Then right at the time when a teenager needs friends the most, they died.

Losing them made me afraid of intimacy, afraid of getting close to someone for fear of having them taken away. I became good at making friends, just not very good at keeping them. If I could set the terms of how close we could be, I was fine. But drift into that "sisterhood" zone, and I would back away in a heartbeat.

When I got older, I came to understand making new friends can be a struggle for working moms, and it's not easy to keep the ones you make. It was extra hard for me because I was on the road. Any spare time back in Tennessee was spent soaking up time with the kids, doing their laundry, and filling their hungry bellies. If you're not living in a social neighborhood or active in a church, it's almost impossible to develop healthy relationships.

Friendships were a problem for me for years. I'd be on the road for weeks at a time, come back for a few days, and friends in the neighborhood or ladies at church would expect me to pick right back up with them. I could barely get to my own kids' birthday parties, much less their kids' events. They'd bring their children to Chera's sleepovers or Zach's parties when I was home, but when they'd ask me to come for little Susie's 8th birthday, I'd be somewhere on Interstate 465 in Indiana. Eventually, people stopped asking.

At other times, when we were in the same place and having an adult conversation, it became clear that my job was completely weird to them. Heck, it's weird to me. I think some of the moms who lived and worked in Murfreesboro thought I was leading some kind of glamorous Hollywood life. While they were packing lunches and volunteering at the school reading program, they assumed I was hobnobbing with stars at the Grand Ole Opry. So they rarely tried to invite me into any of their circles. And then, there were those who invited me to everything merely for the bragging rights for having *the* Chonda Pierce show up at their baby shower—even though no one was pregnant. (True story!)

That reminds me of one of the funniest things my daughter ever said. We were leaving church one morning and a lady stopped Chera and said, "Oh, honey, what does it feel like to have Chonda Pierce as your mother?" Chera gave her a giant fake grin, raised her eyebrows as high as they would go, and said very sarcastically, "Well, sometimes I wake up in the morning and think 'Oh, my God! My mom is Chonda Pierce.'" Then she stomped away. It was so funny, but in retrospect, it might have been a small neon sign.

When you have a job that throws you into any kind of limelight, even if you have only moderate success, you often find out too late that the people who are trading on your name and fame are worse than having a real enemy. At least you can see a real enemy coming. I'd rather be stabbed in the front than in the back.

I am blessed with great girlfriends—most of my circle I have known for over forty years—we graduated from high school together in 1978. They have seen the good, bad, and ugly of Chonda Pierce, and I love them for enduring it all!

Those women taught me a lot about myself and taught me to cherish the friends who had no motive. They don't need a free ticket. They don't care much about my "job." (Well, unless Keith Urban is playing at the Opry the same night I'm there!) These days, I am drawn to the friends who knew me before—before trauma, before grief, before the last fifty-two pounds! Some knew me before I was *Chonda Pierce*, when I was just Chonda Ruth. They're the Girls of '78 that I mentioned awhile back. They are the girls I graduated from high school with in 1978, and here we are—forty-two years later and we've still got each other's backs.

Meribeth is my bestie. She's a banker and my best friend, not in that order. She lives in Memphis, and she's the one person I'd call at 3:00 a.m. if I needed a kidney. Lucky for her, she's a different blood type. But when I do call her depressed and despondent in the middle of the night, she knows what to do. That's why women need girlfriends. Men try to fix you; women listen and support you. If I call my brother because I'm having a bad day, his advice will be to tell me to memorize four scriptures. Meribeth will listen for an hour then tell me to have a glass of wine. Okay, that's not completely true! She will say, "Did you take your meds?!" And then she will ask, "Are you allowed to have a glass of wine?" No! But I can't tell you how many times I wake up in the night with the phone still laying on my face, and I can hear Meribeth and her husband Chuck snoring on the other end!

Meribeth was my first girlfriend when we moved to Tennessee and she still is my very best friend, my boo, my bae, my BFF. (See how young and hip I still am?) Meribeth and I share so much history. She was there when my sisters passed. She knew of my deepest struggles with my dad, and some days she knows me better than I know myself. Meribeth is about the only person I allow to smack my phone out of my hand or knock me on the back of the head when I'm not paying attention. "Stop crushing candy. Be present." She can look at me and know if danger is swirling around in my head. I can keep a straight face while glancing out the window at a speedboat, and she will stare me straight in the face without saying a word, and I know she's thinking, "No, you cannot get one of those."

Once, we were leaving St. Thomas Island with the Girls after a great week of sitting around the pool, playing cards, and shopping. (I know, I am blessed beyond measure!) Somehow, the six of us got separated as we walked through customs to enter the good ole USA.

Okay, *I* got separated. As they were frustratedly waiting for me to make it through, Patrice said to the group, "Wonder what's taking Chonda so long?" Meribeth calmly replied, "She must have told them about that watch, the earrings, and the seven coconuts in her suitcase." How did she even know I had secretly stuffed those coconuts in my suitcase?

I pride myself on knowing I was the only girlfriend Meribeth's folks allowed to stay over on a school night. I think they thought having a preacher's daughter in the house was going to be a good influence on Meribeth. Boy, were they wrong! The minute they closed the door, we'd open the window, shimmy down to the ground, and go out to raise a little hell. I mean . . . to be a fine witness for the Lord Jesus! Remember, there wasn't much hell to raise in our small town. We only had two traffic lights and one of them would flash after 11:00 p.m. There was only one cow, and by 9:00 p.m. she had already been tipped. Besides, my dad was the hellfire-and-brimstone preacher in town, and Meribeth's dad was the most well-known bus driver and Ag teacher in our high school. We didn't have a chance to raise much of anything.

I'll never forget the time Meribeth and I snuck out and met her cousin Betty Nell and my sister Cheralyn. Betty Nell Binkley was my little sister's best friend, and her father was the sheriff in town. We were seniors and they were freshmen. We had convinced them they had to go through a very secret and private orientation in order to hang out with seniors at the high school. This orientation was to take place in the city graveyard. We got a ladder and all climbed on top of a giant mausoleum. Then Meribeth and I told them we would be right back with snacks. Instead, we took the ladder away and left them up there screaming for two hours. Okay, it probably felt like two hours to them, but I think it was more like thirty minutes. After all, we had a curfew. Bottom line, we didn't raise hell, we raised heck.

Several years ago, we lost Betty Nell. Meribeth and I sat with her at the hospital for hours. It was a devastating blow for our little circle of girlfriends. We had just spent a fun weekend in Nashville. I had moved into my tiny apartment. David was rehabbing, and my high school girls knew I needed some "fall apart" time. I didn't even have enough chairs for all of us to sit on, and I barely had enough floor space for sleeping, but I don't think we even closed our eyes for a few minutes. We hadn't all been together in way too many years, so we had lots of catching up to do, tons of laughing to do, and even a little crying here and there.

There was never too much crying when Betty Nell was around though. She was downright hysterical, as country as cornbread, and I could write a book about all the crazy predicaments she got herself into. At the same time, she was the personal assistant for Senator Howard Baker from Tennessee for more than thirty years. I'm pretty sure Betty Nell's sense of humor is why he lived so long. She was funny with a capital F. As matter of fact, the first time she met Andrew Tenenbaum, she put her arm around him and said, "Now, let's cut to the chase. How 'bout drop that blonde chick and make me a superstar. You can be my manager."

About a week after our time in Nashville, Betty Nell had an aneurysm and never recovered. Since that tragedy, the Girls of '78 have become more and more focused and dedicated to staying in touch with calls, social media, and our girls' trips.

The rest of the Girls of '78 is Necie, a biologist; Kim is a lobbyist; and Patrice runs a pharmacy. (Patrice was widowed a long time ago after only three years of marriage. Her children were very small. Her insight was so valuable in my grief.) And then we have our "add-ons" post 1978. Melanie runs a restaurant, Glynda is a retired schoolteacher, Julie is a circuit court clerk, and Karyn Williams is my dearest tour mate. Throw in my very own movie star, Judith Hoag, and I will be the first to tell you—I am indeed incredibly blessed.

When David was going downhill, the girls were there. They made me reconnect, forced me out of my funk, and demanded I hang out with them. They're real friends, not social media friends. Yes, we do connect on social media, but we talk in person and on the phone. Let's be honest, if you have five thousand Facebook friends with no phone numbers, chances are you can't consider any of them real friends. Real friends are those who have seen you cry, who know your secrets but would never divulge them. They know who you were, who you are, and where you just don't need to be, yet will walk beside you to make sure you don't take that journey alone. They have taken the sting out of widowhood for me. It is thanks to them that I am in a place to write this book. So, if you have any complaints about it, call them!

Crazy thing is, I can read an audience of thousands—but I am notorious for not having the greatest judgement when it comes to hiring folks, dating folks, or even scrolling through Angie's List. I will always pick the oddest bird.

Not that long ago, I started telling Meribeth about an old acquaintance that I had gone to dinner with. I'm sure she was more than suspicious of the tone of my giddy voice. I prattled on and on, "Wouldn't it be just really something if I wind up with him? I mean, I have known him for thirty years. He knows everything about this business. I mean, he's on parole, but it's just nine more years." Meribeth very nonchalantly listened and nodded her head while she scrolled through pictures on my phone and read our text exchanges. She very calmly handed me my phone as she said, "No, Chonda. It's not going to happen. He's got some stuff to work out. A lot to work out. Bring it down. Step away." Hours later I was glancing through my phone and noticed no more text messages, no pictures . . . she had replaced his number for hers and had put her goofy face where every picture had been saved. Oddly, I didn't get angry, frustrated, or disappointed. I trust her, AND she reminded me of about four other times I hired farmhands and merchandise folks that became a mess to get rid of!

Between Meribeth and Zachary—I have great screeners. I almost feel sorry for the man who they will interrogate to simply take me out for a glass of sweet tea. I'm pretty sure that Meribeth and Zachary will be the ones that walk me down the aisle if I ever get married again. Well, Zach will. Meribeth will be busy holding the shotguns! And by the way, Meribeth gets Zachary in my will. They deserve each other!

# CHAPTER 18

# DATING FOR DUMMIES

I have made it pretty clear that I will never get married again, but after concerts, people still often ask me if I'm dating again. I probably have some displaced loyalty to David. (Note to self: Call Tracey, the therapist, on this one!) He's been gone since 2014, and I miss him every day. And I miss the "you know what." The sex. Or as Mom would say, "the Sunday night roast." I hope my kids read this part. They will throw up in their mouths a little.

I know some people will be shocked that I used that word. Not roast, *sex*. But think about it, if you are living on this planet, and you are reading this book now, chances are somebody in your family's past had sex. At least once. Might not have been the best thirty seconds in their life, but they did it.

See—right there. I went a little too edgy. Well, that's what some emails from a few church ladies say. Truth is, I wasn't always so blunt. I played it so safe that I even felt bored with me. Several years ago, I was working away—in the comedy biz we say, "I was on a roll." I knew in my head what I was going to say next, talk about the roast, tiptoe around the obvious, but still try to find a way to make it funny. I looked out at my audience—98 percent were women close to my age, and maybe a few younger. There were three or four terrified men in the back and about three teenage girls that probably knew more about this subject than their mothers would like to think. So, I said it. "*Sex!* I miss sex." Honestly, the reaction of the crowd was hysterical. It woke everybody up! We roared laughing at ourselves. The world has gone bonkers with this "woke" generation. But I think there are a few things the church crowd could stand to get woke about as well.

Back to dating . . .

The answer is, yes, I try to date. It's been a long time since my very first date ever—Gerald Ford was president—and my current dating life is just as clumsy. Now? Now, it is downright horrible at my age. They say it's like riding a bicycle, which means to me there's a chance one of us will fall off and someone needs to wear a helmet for protection. I never dreamed I'd be dating all over again at forty-five-ish. (I'm not under oath, right?) Online dating is tough because the world is full of stinking, lying men. Wait, that's redundant. I'm kidding. Kind of.

The worst part of online dating is that the men you meet in person do not look like their picture. The men I meet are like a Denny's burger. There's no way the burger that arrives on your plate even remotely resembles the perfectly cooked, beautifully arranged meal on the menu photo. Fill in your own disappointing buns joke.

Occasionally, I see a cute one. I know, some of the Christian women reading this are shaking their heads. Come on! It's okay to say a man is cute. You know, like that cute pastor at church who made the sermons a lot more fun to look at, I mean listen to. You know the one I mean. You don't go to church for a year, your best friend tells you about how mesmerizing the new pastor is, so you go one Sunday and find out he looks like Brad Pitt. At that point you not only go to church every Sunday, you start asking for Saturday morning services too.

And the worst part about dating again is trying to decide how many pairs of Spanx to put on. Is this guy a two pair or three pair? It's a math equation: cuteness of date factored by the type of food at the restaurant. Let me explain: An unattractive guy at a sushi restaurant, one pair. Really cute guy at the Cheesecake Factory, I'll have to squeeze into three pairs before the date and use the Jaws of Life to extract myself afterwards.

I think marriage evolved so women wouldn't have to get dolled up for dates. I hate getting dolled up. If you ever see me on a stage and I look a little dolled up, appreciate the effort, will ya? It is not my favorite part of the night. Good thing my husband liked me just the way I am, and it got even better the older he got and the worse his eyesight became. I was always hot to him. Nowadays my only hot comes in flashes.

At first, dating again made me feel angry at David for deciding to go to heaven first. Two great songs come to mind about a spouse that dies first. Collin Raye's "If You Get There Before I Do" and Brad Paisley's "Waiting on a Woman." One will make you cry and the other will make you smile, but they both comfort me when I focus on the fact that David died before me. Later, the few dates I had were just sad. When you read people for a living, it can truly interfere with reading a semi-stranger across the table. One man worked frantically to convince me he was a great catch. "Frank" had been married four times. He went on to tell me what he learned about each wife, what was wrong with each of them, and now he was convinced that a woman like me would be the most fun wife on the planet! I asked him, "Frank, what do you think is the common denominator in all those marriages?" He looked at me curiously. "Hmm, well, they were all women?" (I guess that's good to know in this day and age!)

"No, Frank. *You* are the common denominator in those marriages, Frank!" We never went out again.

Which raises the question, am I looking for the perfect man to date to replace David? Am I trying to find a new love to replace my soulmate? Yes, I am, although he doesn't exist. But I know exactly who he should be. He's the man who has invented a type of fried chicken and ice cream I can eat without having it go right to my hips.

My friends ask if I miss conjugal relations, which sounds like I'm in prison. "She's been on good behavior so we're allowing her a visit to have conjugal relations." I'm not sure what it will be like to be intimate again. The movies make it all so ridiculously romantic. I'm sixty-three at the time of writing this, and sex seems about as interesting as a good book and hot bath. It is intimacy that I miss. Sex approached casually, well, it's just that—casual. But intimacy—that lasts longer. It is the beautiful part of preparing a roast, cooking the roast, and simply enjoying being together. Yes, I miss that.

Nevertheless, my posse, my wing women, the Girls of '78 nudged me to sign up for online dating. And I'm smart. I posted a photo of Phyllis Diller so when the guys see me in person, they'll think, "Darn, she's not a three. She's a solid four."

My online dating profile reads, "Slim blonde, closer to age 40 than she is to 30 (that one is true), runs five times a week (does it count if I run to the counter at Dairy Queen?), looking for a man who has money and a pulse."

I may not ever win an Emmy, but I could win the Pulitzer Prize for fiction.

The first site I tried was eHarmony. Big mistake. It's a wonderful company, but the paperwork is too complicated with its twenty-nine dimensions of compatibility. By the time I was done, Dr. Neil Clark Warren was probably saying there's someone for everyone except

Chonda. After reading over all my answers, I decided I wouldn't want to date me.

I considered FarmersOnly.com but ruled it out, as I have never been a big fan of bib overalls. Besides, I have a farm and I think my own tractor is sexy!

I did go on ChristianMingle. Not very Christian, way too much mingling. Plus, I found out some of the men there already have a wife. If this were Utah in 1885, okay, but Nashville in 2023? Not good.

Then there is that cheap website, Plenty of Fish. I asked one of the men there what he used to lure the fish, and he sent me a picture. You can probably guess what the picture was. I knew immediately he wasn't Jewish. Why would a man send a picture of that? Don't you know that stuff never goes away? You can find that picture on Hunter Biden's laptop if Congress ever decided to do any questioning or investigating. Do you really want your junk displayed on CNN? Don't answer that. A man who would send you a picture like that probably would.

I ruled out Tinder. I could never remember whether I'm supposed to swipe right or left . . . plus it's embarrassing to do it on one of those Jitterbug phones.

I did sign up on OurTime, that dating site for singles over fifty. First, my profile photo looked much younger than most of the men I saw on there. Second, dating someone much older would make me look like a "kept" woman. That sounded wonderful to me, until I realized I would probably be kept in a nursing home with Fred. Fred's profile picture was of himself sitting on the side of a bed in a hospital gown with an oxygen tube under his nose. I kid you *not*. I gave up OurTime and opted for some ME Time! Besides, if I'm getting another car, it's going to be a new Porsche, not a used Chevette.

One woman suggested I consider dating someone who was just coming out of prison. The idea was if prison didn't reform him, maybe

I could. That was the dumbest idea ever. What would I tell my friends? I'm dating a new guy. #536754. His online photo is a mugshot. Like I am going to date a felon. Although if he was a bank robber, and they never found the money and he still had it, who I am not to forgive a reformed sinner?

As much as I joke about it, online dating is better than friends trying to match me up with their cousin.

"Chonda, you've got to meet Jim Bob. He's a real catch. Sixty years old. Never been married. Such a good son, he lives with his momma. Been out of work for a few years since the big recession. Of 1978."

Seriously? If a guy is sixty, lives with his mama, and has never been married, there's a reason. It's a fine reason, but I'm going to guess he's on the other team.

Not that I'm an expert, but I must wonder what some of these men are doing in their photos. Posing with your shirt off when you need to wear a bigger bra than me is not a good idea. Even worse are the men who take selfies in the bathroom while they are sitting on the toilet. What were they thinking? "Man, I look like a stud muffin today. I bet I look even better sitting on the commode."

But if creating a profile is bad, and swiping right is bad, the actual date is even worse. I am not ready for 2023 dating. Especially since I have some measure of fame—no one will pick up the check. No one. Wait, I'm wrong, there was a guy named Bob. We went to a very expensive restaurant in Nashville, and he picked up the check—then handed it to me.

I'm fine with a split check, but the guys I date think split means 90/10. Their idea of half is when I take the half with the signature.

I spent almost thirty-two years with a great man. We fell in love at sixteen, and that love grew into an amazing and creative relationship. We came from just about nothing, and through the mercy of God, we held on when most couples would have walked away from each other. We learned from tough mistakes, but what I didn't learn enough about in all those years was *me*.

There is a scene in the movie *Runaway Bride*. Julia Roberts had left at least four men at the altar. At one point, Richard Gere challenges her about this very subject. In writing an article about her character, he notices that with every fella, she always ordered her eggs how the men liked them. Near the end of the movie, she finally cooks eggs—scrambled, over easy, eggs benedict, poached . . . until she decides what *she* likes.

A lone tear ran down my face watching that scene.

That's me. Okay, not the size two glamour millionaire actress who dumps Richard Gere at the altar. David and I were on and off for seven years. More on than off. Then married, and within the first year started a family. Soon windows and doors started flying open for me to do what I do. All wonderful. All blessed. But underneath it all, I didn't know *me* like I needed to. But I'm getting there. I discovered I like my eggs scrambled with cheese and a tablespoon of salsa on top, by the way. And I know this about me—I WILL SURVIVE.

In fact, I came up with my own words to "I Will Survive." When I met Gloria Gaynor, we had a great laugh with my version.

At first, I was afraid, I was mortified
Kept thinking I would get a treadmill when I turned
forty-five
But then I spent so many nights eating all those Krispy
Kremes
That I could see I'd never fit in my blue jeans

And so I'm back on NordicTrack
I just walk miles I get nowhere trying to burn up all this fat
I shoulda changed to Pepsi-free, cottage cheese, and celery
If I had known for just one second there'd be so much more
of me

Oh no not I, I'm satisfied
I don't care if I will never be a size two in my life
I've got all this life to live and I've got all this love to give
I'm satisfied, I'm satisfied, hey, hey

Silly little rice cakes won't pass through my lips
I want chocolate covered donuts hanging on my hips
Cause I spent oh so many nights trying to starve myself
But oh, not I—now I always supersize

And you can see,
There's more of me
I'm not that scrawny little girl that I used to be
Fried foods and double chins are still a girl's best friend
Keep those models on the runway
Cause I'm a perfect ten

Oh no not I, I'm satisfied
I don't care if I will never be a size four in my life
Oh no not I, I'm satisfied
I don't care if I will never be a size six in my life
Oh no not I, I'm satisfied
I don't care if I will never be a size eight in my life
I've got all this life to live and I've got all this love to give
I'm satisfied, I'm satisfied, hey, hey

The last date I had a few years ago, the man swore up and down that he didn't mind if I was famous. My job really didn't matter. He's never really been a fan of comedy, and he is never intimidated by strong women. If he said it once, he said it ten times. Yet, before he said goodbye, he said, "Mind if I grab a picture with you? I can't wait to tell my friends I took Chonda Pierce out for dinner." Sigh.

At the time of writing this chapter, I have kind of given up on dating. One of my favorite girlfriends on the planet for many years was Patsy Bruce. She is in Heaven now, but I really feel like it was a divine appointment when she became my neighbor for almost seven years during my widow recovery time. She was one of the strongest and wisest women. She was a famous Nashville songwriter. Her most famous song was "Mammas Don't Let Your Babies Grow Up to be Cowboys." One evening she told me to stop looking and searching for a man. "God knows right where you are," she said. "Besides, if the Lord can part the Red Sea, He can put a man on your porch."

About three weeks later, I heard a clamor on the balcony of my condo. I pushed open the curtains only to discover not one but three very handsome Hispanic men standing on my balcony. I grabbed the phone and called Patsy. "God has overdone it! He sent Shadrach, Meshach, and Abednego." Before I could snap a picture, they had already repelled down to the next windows to wash.

## CHAPTER 19

# WINNERS AND WHINERS

"Welcome to the Grand Ole Opry!"

That's always the first line out of the emcee's mouth as the red velvet curtain rises to reveal that big red barn behind a few church pews and one of the best country bands in music history. The stage of the Opry is one of my favorite places to stand in the world. I am grateful every time I am asked to perform there.

For anyone who has been on that stage, it's an extraordinary honor. If you're a baseball player, you want to compete in the World Series; if you're an opera singer, you want to sing at Lincoln Center; and if you're a country performer, you dream of standing on the country's most famous stage.

My first invitation came in 1995 when I was a brand-new comic. The general manager of the Opry, Bob Whitaker (my old boss), was proud of every young performer's rise to fame who had started in the theme parks. Since then, I have been blessed to perform there about a hundred times. (Actually, I lost count, but a hundred sounds good to me!) But my first time performing there is the one night I'll never forget. I was so excited and nervous. I performed a lot of material from my very first project "Second Row, Piano Side." Actually, it was the only material I had at the time!

In case you are not familiar with the Grand Ole Opry, it is the longest-running radio show in history. So, while performers stand on the stage doing their thing in front of several thousand people, the entire planet can tune in via the famous WSM radio network. The stage show is broken up into thirty-minute segments complete with commercial breaks most often done by the emcee or Opry backup singers on stage. During my first time, the famous Connie Smith (a member of the Opry since 1965) introduced me, and out I stepped in front of thousands of faces. Honestly, my hands still shake typing this. But I did it! I made it to the Grand Ole Opry. My heart swells right now just thinking about it.

Maybe it's because I got my start in comedy because of Cousin Minnie Pearl. Maybe it's because I have been in Nashville most of my life, and it is the measure of hard work and success in my town. Whatever that butterfly is that flutters around your memory, it was a magical, unforgettable night for me. Funny, I think David was even more nervous than I was that night! He bought a new dress shirt, and I wore a new dress for the occasion. Bob Whitaker even had a limo pick us up and drive us to the backstage entrance.

As we began to walk out the door after my performance, Connie Smith stopped us in the hall and asked if I could stay a few minutes longer. "Marty Stuart just heard you on the radio and wants to come meet you," she said.

"No," I said. "Sorry, we're kind of hungry and need to go get the kids." Ha! Of course, I did not say that! We were thrilled. *The* Marty Stuart is a presence, I must say. He swaggers into a room with enough glitz, glamour, and class to make a Kardashian look like a floozy. Come to think of it, I think they are a bit floozy completely on their own. Nevertheless, Marty Stuart came swaggering down the hall in his cowboy boots, surrounded by people grabbing at him, asking for autographs (yep, he's a legend). Connie graciously introduced us, and I was stunned as he grabbed my hand and pulled me into the nearest dressing room, away from the crowded hallway. Then, he pulled a dollar bill out of his wallet and signed it. He handed it to me and said, "Chonda, this is the first dollar of your first million 'cause you're gonna be a damn star!" He has no idea how many times we have almost had to take that dollar out of its frame and use it.

Hilariously, we almost had to spend that dollar on our way home. We asked the limo driver if he could take us to the drive-through window at Krystal. (You know, those tiny square burgers.) David had five dollars in his wallet, I had $2.43—not including the autographed bill. We whispered to each other that Krystal would be the cheapest, which would leave the five-dollar bill to tip the limo driver. We munched on our two tiny burgers and shared fries as the limo rolled into our little neighborhood. When David pulled five bucks from his wallet, the driver said, "No, need. Bob Whitaker took care of that." (If we had known that, then we would have gotten a large Coke!) Thankfully, Marty Stuart's dollar is still in a frame on a shelf in my office.

It's unlikely I will ever receive a Grammy. That doesn't bother me. I've never won a Dove Award from the Gospel Music Association. That's okay; they don't even know I sing. But for me, the Opry has been my hope, my goalpost for more than thirty years. I still get butterflies when they call. I am always mesmerized by its iconic importance. There have been few comics inducted as members of the Opry. Only one was a woman: Sarah Cannon, the real Cousin Minnie Pearl. To the best of my knowledge, there have been very few female comics even to be invited to perform at the Opry since Miss Minnie's passing. The focus there, of course, is country music, but comedy has always been a great pause in the show there. I suppose that is why I feel doubly honored and always keep my eye on that goal.

As I scrolled through my Facebook feed several months ago, an announcement popped up. The newest members to be asked to join the Grand Ole Opry were not one but *two* comics: Gary Mule Deer and Henry Cho. Don't get me wrong. They are both very funny. Very hardworking. Very deserving. But my heart sank. They could have simply punched me in the gut. It hurt my feelings so badly that I could hardly breathe. I called my manager in tears. "What do I have to do? I have tried to be available when they call. I have Gold records, Platinum records. I get the laughs every time. Miss Minnie was my friend. I just don't get it." And on and on and on. I was devastated. Correction, I wasn't devastated; I was ridiculous. I was being a big old silly crybaby, seething with envy and jealousy. I took out my phone and texted Henry Cho a sincere (well, almost) "Congrats, dear friend." I am completely embarrassed to say I sulked around the house for days. The goalpost didn't only move, it was ripped down by the opposing team and carried off the field.

Bobby Bare sang a hilarious country song in 1976 called "Dropkick Me Jesus" in which he pleads, "Dropkick me, Jesus, through the goal-posts of life." Yep, God just kicked me right through the uprights! I think God lets these things happen for a myriad of reasons. First, I was humbled really quick, as in seconds. Second, I think—no, I know—I've had the wrong goal for too long. As much as I dream about it, as much as I want it, becoming a member of the Opry may never happen because that might not be God's goal for me. I have asked Him a dozen times, "Then what *is* the plan, God? What are *your* career goals for me, Lord?" (I know, I know—you know the answer. I know the answer. But, once in a while, you know that I know we still ask! Whew! That's a lot of "knowing and not knowing.")

The Bible says, "Take delight in the Lord, and he will give you the desires of your heart" (Psalm 37:4). Okay, check. I have taken delight. I have shared the good news. However, the Bible also says, "For where your treasure is, there your heart will be also" (Luke 12:34). *Ouch*!

I once heard a comic say, "God can turn water into wine, but He can't do anything with your whining!" Yes, even after all I've been through, after all the hard lessons learned, I'm a whiner! I look back and see how often my "treasure" was found at the end of the wrong rainbow, the wrong pot of gold, or the wrong goalpost. But today, if you ask me where my treasures are in this life, what my career goals are, they are so much more simple, so much more heavenly minded. My home and getting the laundry done. Seeing my son walking in step with Jesus. My sanity—a goal that keeps me extra busy! And then there is treasure. I have great treasures from my career that have nothing to do with trophies and bling on the wall.

One of my greatest treasures is Branches Recovery Center in Murfreesboro, Tennessee—a place that was birthed out of great pain. (I almost chuckle at the commercial we could have made for television, "Branches—Not only a place for healing. But I'm a patient too!") My brother did so much to build this place into the amazing facility that it is. It is a place where my brother and I can both say, "Look what God has done with our broken lives."

I think my entire life is a testament to this verse. "God will work all things for good" (a paraphrase of Romans 8:28). Because out of the trauma, tragedies, and downright ugly messes I've made, occasionally, life evens out and good things emerge.

When I came home from the psychiatric hospital in the year 2000, David had gotten an offer to teach English at Middle Tennessee State University, and he didn't want to leave me alone in our house, which I can understand. The river was getting high, and David wasn't sure if I was still thinking about jumping. So, every morning before he went to work, he would drop me off at my brother's house so someone could babysit me. They didn't live anywhere near the river, and there were no better caregivers than Mike and Doris. They each took turns reading scripture and praying, and sometimes Doris would play a beautiful hymn on the piano. I could hear the words in my head, and they would drown out the negative thoughts that had taken up residence there. They're the kind of voices that beat you down and keep you awake.

For some reason, I could sleep at Mike's house. Maybe it was hearing the soothing voice of my big brother as he read the scriptures, maybe it was the sound of his snoring, but either way, being around my hero comforted me, and each day I would wake up just a little more refreshed, a little stronger.

On one of the last days I spent at their house, I fell asleep as Mike read his Bible. I don't know how long I slept, but for the first time in a long time, I dreamed. Not just any dream. A wonderful dream. It was almost like a vision, so real, so vivid that I sat straight up on the couch and started describing it to Mike and Doris.

In my dream, David and I were outside a large building pulling weeds in a flowerbed, talking and smiling and laughing. Then I looked up through a giant picture window where Mike and Doris and their sons sat inside at a long conference table next to some faces I didn't recognize. Occasionally, I would stop pulling weeds with David and interrupt the meeting where Mike was discussing care groups and what rooms to put people in. Everyone was brainstorming ideas for helping specific groups of people. Divorce Care. Depression

Care. AA/Al-Anon. Next to the building, I noticed a single tree with long branches stretching across the lawn. Inscribed on one long branch that swept across the lawn was the verse, "I am the vine, you are the branches" (John 15:5).

As I recounted the dream with every detail to Mike and Doris, they both began to cry. They said for the first time in months my voice was alive and clear and energetic, as opposed to the low, weak monotone of a depressed person.

I told them I needed to paint what I saw in my dream. I'm not much of a painter, although I had been trying to learn for years, and David had given me an art easel complete with paints and brushes. I called him and asked him to bring it over. That evening, while it was fresh in my memory, I stood and painted the tree, the window, and the long branch stretching across the lawn.

Weeks later, we resumed the Bible study my brother had been teaching in his home. My living room was bigger, so we moved to my house. It was a fun group of folks, and my brother is an excellent teacher. One evening, over the coffeepot and donuts (because if you're going to study the Bible, you must serve donuts; it's in the Old Testament in the Book of Dunkin), a man who was relatively new to the group walked up to Mike and mentioned that he heard Mike was looking for a building to move the Bible study into. My brother said, "No, not really! Haven't been thinking about it." But this man insisted that Mike look at a vacant property he had.

My phone rang the next day. "Chonda, you and David need to get in the car right now and come look at this," my brother's voice was filled with excitement. He gave us the directions to an empty building. "Turn left by White Castle, go past the hotel, and cross Freedom Street."

I gasped as David and I pulled up to the building. I felt like I had been here before. An empty building with an overgrown flowerbed across the front in great need of weeding. It was exactly like the one in my dream. Talk about a neon sign from God!

My brother had been working at various jobs for a while. His phone rang from time to time with an invitation to preach or share his story. (Did I tell you Mike wrote a book? It's a powerful story!) David and I were recovering financially from our latest manager fiasco, and I was still recovering emotionally and physically from deep clinical depression. But on that day, somehow, some way, we all knew it: We knew we had to turn that building into something meaningful. We had no money to put down on it, but the owner—I think he knew it too—insisted we use the building rent-free for a couple months.

We cleaned and weeded and painted. Doris and I spent hours going from one salvage store to another buying desks, chairs, and couches. David and Mike did the painting, and we all spent days cleaning and preparing for something. And honestly, we weren't quite sure what we were preparing for.

We had no idea who would walk in or what the place would become. We laughed and shook our heads, wondering if it was the craziest thing we had ever done. We turned one big room into a chapel for our Bible study and decided to use the other offices for small groups and counseling. Mike would be our only counselor.

After the first week, we opened a little library in one room where we collected resource books. If you have a library, you need a librarian, so we put my mom in charge and named her "the one and only chief and head librarian."

Then came the day. We mounted a sign in "Branches Recovery Center" and established a Bible study, AA meetings, and a variety of help groups.

Every day seemed miraculous beyond words. People started showing up—more and more every day. People looking for group meetings, folks in need of counseling, many sharing their stories with us. Most had similar experiences to what my brother or I had walked through. There were overcomers working to stay on the right path. Recovering addicts. Marriages on the brink of disaster. It became apparent that we were walking a pathway illuminated every single day by the greatest visionary, God Himself. We felt blessed and overwhelmed, and we were in way over our heads!

Then one day, a young woman pulled in. She introduced herself, saying she saw the sign and something told her to stop. Tracey Robinson was a clinical director at Vanderbilt University, a licensed counselor, and was looking for a new place to work. Fate? Coincidence? God's hand at work? I'll go with door #3. My brother and I almost laughed, not at her, but at the sheer goodness of God. At that point, we weren't surprised a bit!

Branches Recovery Center grew rapidly over the years and ultimately became Branches Counseling Center. My brother was CEO of five facilities that make up a faith-based counseling center that offers healing and hope for those struggling with depression, anxiety, addiction, and shame. And we offer that help regardless of anyone's ability to pay. Our staff includes licensed and pastoral counselors, doctors, therapists, nutrition specialists, you name it. Branches provides help to couples, individuals, adults, children, and teens. The idea is simple—we bring traditional counseling and Biblical principles to people struggling with personal, family, and relationship issues—individuals looking for support through the toughest times in their lives. Although I have little to do with the day-to-day operations, I am proud of Branches and the work there.

For all the lamenting I have done about never witnessing a miracle and all the whining over career disappointments, when I see the board meeting minutes or the new budget for the year from Branches, I see the growth. The center treats thousands of patients. The weight loss clinic has received a myriad of awards. It is thriving, booming. It is our trophy. Yes, the whining stops.

Recently, Branches hosted a retirement party for my brother. Mike was passing the mantle to his oldest son. A great big wall displayed photos, accomplishments, professional accolades, awards, and testimonials from all around the world, and over in the corner under a tiny pin light was the painting I painted over twenty years ago.

I am reminded of Psalm 37, "Commit your way to the Lord; trust in him and he will do this: He will make your righteous reward shine like the dawn, your vindication like the noon day sun. Be still before the Lord and wait patiently for him; do not fret when people succeed in their ways" (vv. 5–7).

I think I kicked the ball right down the middle of the goalposts. God is good.

## CHAPTER 20

# MUSICAL CASKETS

Ten years after my parents' divorce, my mother remarried a wonderful man named Samuel. Mom called him Sam, but I called him Papaw. He was a simple man who worked in a factory for fifty years, got a gold watch when he retired, then went back to work bagging groceries at Kroger for another ten years. He was nothing like my dad. But oh, how that man adored my mother.

Sam was also an usher at church, and he called my brother one day to ask if he could take my mom out for Sunday dinner. When I asked Mike how he responded to him, he said, "You can take her to Tahiti if you want. We don't care!" We laughed, Sam took Mom to Sunday dinner, and they were married four months later.

It was a sweet wedding on a Saturday afternoon at church with only family present. Afterward, they got personalized license plates. Samuel's plate read, "I LUV VA," and Mom's read, "I LUV SAM." They were two peas in a pod. And from that day forward, they did everything together. I used to laugh often and say, "If there were ever a prize for the best purse-carrying hubby, Papaw would win—hands down."

They usually drove to church separately because Papaw had to be there early as an usher. Both were notorious for following much too close to the car in front of them. One Sunday on their way home, Mother must have stopped abruptly, and Sam plowed into the back of her car right in front of a policeman coming from the opposite direction. Of course, the traffic lined up quickly and the policeman began to fill out the proper paperwork. The story goes, he wrote mom's plate number down very slowly, reading the letters deliberately, "I-L-U-V-S-A-M." He looked at Papaw and said, "She's not who I think she is, is she?" Papaw said, "Yep! That's my wife, and I am Sam."

Mother had been alone just over ten years after she and my dad divorced. For many years before Mom met Sam, I was the caretaker of all things Mother. When she faced breast cancer, I took her to every appointment, every chemotherapy treatment. Although Sammy was a remarkable comfort and love for Mother, she depended greatly on me for just about everything. Most of the time, I didn't mind. Most of the time. But often, being newly married and raising a toddler clashed with Mother's codependency on her adult children.

My brother was living in Ohio during most of that time, but after he came back to Tennessee, Sam took a liking to Mike, always seeking out his advice. He wouldn't even open the mail without running it by Mike. It was so sweet, but Mike was perplexed by it. He once told me, "I didn't sign up to inherit Papaw." I just grinned back at him and said, "Look, I had them for thirty years before you came back to Tennessee, so now it's your turn!"

My mom died while David was still living. She and Sam wanted both of their names on the same tombstone. My sisters' heart-shaped tombstones were the same, and they had been placed side by side in the cemetery. The stone for Mother and Sam was taller in order to fit both names on it. It did not look symmetrical beside Charlotta's and Cheralyn's. It bugged me every time I took flowers to their gravesites.

So, one night after driving home from the cemetery, I told David I wanted to plant some azaleas there, and I didn't like how the tombstones were arranged next to each other. I wished we had thought to put Mother's stone in between my sisters' stones. Like a good Tennessee redneck husband, David replied, "I'll wait 'til it gets dark..."

Later that night, David loaded a heavy chain into his Jeep and drove to the cemetery. He used the chain to separate my sisters' tombstones and pull Mom's stone in between them. They were beautifully symmetrical, with the taller stone in the middle between two heart-shaped ones. It looked perfect, even though Mom's body was on the left, under Charlotta's name, and Charlotta's body was under Cheralyn's name (I don't really know how that happened!). Mom's name was in the middle—that's all I know—and my ADHD could subside a bit. I chuckled to myself at the thought of the Second Coming and the musical chairs they would play in the cemetery!

David died two years after my mom and, as much as my mother loved David and as much as David loved her, I was always worried about resurrection morning. If my mother was the first face he saw, he might want to wait until *after* the tribulation! Besides, I knew exactly what he would love the most! The Funny Farm. I knew he would be at peace there.

Papaw died in 2021. It broke our hearts. He was such a dear and sweet connection to my mother. He held a very tender spot in my brother's heart. Mike had grown so fond of that simple man who called him his son. I loved him so much, not just as a father I had always wanted, but as an amazing grandfather. The grandkids loved and accepted him completely. After a brief graveside service, Johnny Jones, the funeral director for everyone in my family, motioned us over. His daughter, Teresa, had already texted me earlier, "The minute you get to the cemetery, meet me in the corner. We need to talk." I just thought I'd catch up to her graveside.

Mike and I rallied with Teresa and her father. "What can we do for you? Is there a problem?" Teresa quipped, "Oh yes. There is a problem."

"Papaw can't stay here," she said.

"What do you mean?" I asked. They had already placed him in a hole next to Cheralyn. "He's dangling over this hole, so what do you mean he can't stay here?"

She said, "This spot belongs to another family. We tried to call them all day long to ask if they would sell it to you, and when we finally got ahold of them, they said no. So tomorrow, we will need to come back up here and move Papaw."

"But he's supposed to be here with Mother," I said pointing to the middle tombstone with their names on it.

"That's the problem," she continued. "They dug a hole there, got to the casket, but that ain't your mama!" I tried to hold my tongue as she said, "Then they tried the next one, and that ain't her either! I don't know what has happened here."

I'm sure my face was bright red as I told her, "Oh. Um. Well, a few months ago, I had my husband come and rearrange the stones so they would look more symmetrical, more artistic and beautiful."

We all tried keeping our composure in front of the few onlookers still standing around Papaw's body being lowered into his temporary hole. Teresa continued, "Well, these boys aren't going to dig another hole in 100-degree weather again, I can't ask them to. And there is too much bedrock to put him where your mother's body is. Do you want to just find another family in the cemetery that will take Papaw?"

"Just put him with Charlotta. What does it matter? Just put him where his name is even though he'll be on top of Charlotta. Cemeteries stack people all the time, don't they?"

"We can't do that. There is so much bedrock here, we can't dig any deeper. If we try to put him next to your mama, we would have to pull her out and use a jackhammer to dig deep enough. And you don't want your mama out in this heat."

By this time, we were all laughing so hard because this would only happen to us. They suggested we find another spot somewhere else in the cemetery, but I said, "No, we need to keep the family together. I think we should just put him in with Charlotta."

Mike spoke up then and said, "That's where I draw the line, Chonda. You can't put him there. They don't even know each other!"

"You know," I said, "I think this is as good a time as any. Let's move them all! Let's pull them all up and take them out to the farm and bury them with David."

The next morning, the funeral workers loaded all the caskets onto a flatbed trailer behind a two-ton pickup truck because that was the only way four of them would fit. Then they pulled out all of the tombstones and set them with their respective caskets and set off toward the Funny Farm.

I filmed the whole ordeal because Mike couldn't be there that day. Zach rode with me, rolling his eyes while I waved at people as we drove by. When we got close to McDonald's, I turned to Zach and said, "I'll give you five hundred dollars if you drive through and order four cheeseburgers." I guess he just wasn't hungry enough though.

It was the most hilarious day. Police came out to help as if we were a funeral procession. People in cars pulled over, stopped, and got out of their cars and stared at us. They must have thought there had been a mass murder in town. To me, it was the funniest thing I had ever seen. But the funniest part was when we went over the river and through the woods. That sounds cliché, but it's true. We had to drive over the Cumberland River and down a winding road to get to my farm, and the tarp covering the caskets blew off into the river. So then we had one nice, new casket and three muddy ones rattling along on the trailer.

We finally arrived at the farm and lined them all up in order near David. We matched the tombstones with all the right bodies.

I love telling that story because it makes people laugh, but it also reminds me that I have my family all together on my farm. I can see the little cemetery from my front porch. I created a pathway lined with flowers leading to it, and I walk out there with my morning coffee whenever I'm not on the road.

I like to say, "I love that my family is with me on my property because I may have increased the odds of sitting out there when Jesus comes. And since the dead in Christ will rise first, I'll have time to put my lipstick on in case my grandmother sees me coming."

Honestly, it was funny. Until it wasn't. You face your own mortality whenever you face the death of someone close to you. I began to wonder how long it will be before I am buried alongside them. My son always jokes, "Well, I'm just gonna drag you out of the bed and roll you into the hole. It will save time and money!"

Friends have asked, "Are you really comfortable living so close to a cemetery like that?"

My response is, "I absolutely love it." I told my brother that I'd love to find someone who can build me a picnic table around the tree out there so I can sit and have lunch or my morning coffee with my family. Mike doesn't think that's healthy, but I do. I don't know why I'm so comfortable with the idea. When you've faced death often and in so many ways, it's not as big of a deal as people think it is. More than likely, I will get a call from my therapist after she reads this. Maybe I have something to work on. But truthfully, I have become very acquainted with death—I drive past the cemetery every day to go to the grocery store. Coming home from a weekend of shows, I drive by slowly and say, "I'm back!" The stones line up against the evening sky at times and remind me often how short life can be.

I've found that the best way to honor my deceased loved ones is to live well.

I remember the scene in the movie *Twister* where two people run into a toolshed and use a belt to tie themselves to a metal pipe. The tornado is about to pass over them, and when it does, the woman looks up into the middle of it, and it's almost pretty because you can see the sunlight through the center of the funnel. That moment of grief is a lot like that—when you hear the words that someone you love has died and the shock is whistling in your ears, if you are a believer, there can be a moment in the midst of that whirlwind of grief and trying to catch your breath when you can look up and see a little bit of sunlight and be reminded this isn't the end of the story.

I don't know how I will go. I don't plan it. The good Lord, my pastor, doctor, counselor, and the Girls of '78 would be on my porch tomorrow if I said otherwise. No, I'm not planning it. But all I know is that I have strapped myself in for this thing called life. It has been harsh at times, and painful. It has whirled around with great destruction at times. But, sometimes, just sometimes, I have peered up into the middle of the storm to see the beautiful sunlight of God's love and mercy and grace.

# EPILOGUE

I do a lot of things backwards (I know that's a real shock to my faithful fans and readers). I don't know how other comics work it, but before I go out on tour, I always know how I'm going to end my concerts. And once I have the final fifteen minutes in mind, the first hour and forty-five minutes is easy.

I knew how I wanted this book to end before I wrote the first twenty chapters. So much had been bottled up inside me that I just let it all come out, which is why my editor is now in rehab. Now I'm at the end of the book and it's time to wrap it up with a survivor story, but this time, it's not about me. It's about a survivor who inspired me. My mom.

My mother survived a bad marriage to a very broken and unfaithful man, the deaths of two of her daughters, and the struggle to give me a chance at a better life. Heck, my mother survived watching me and my brother muddle through to the other side of recovery.

It gives me sweet comfort to know that Mom was so proud of me. After Papaw died, Mike, Doris, and I went through the house to get it ready to put it up for sale. There was very little of anything valuable in her small house. Mom and Papaw lived very simply. But in every nook and cranny, there were boxes of newspaper clippings, magazine articles, pictures. My brother would go through boxes in the other room and chuckle, "There's more Chonda shrine in here!"

Although Mom did have a way of keeping me in my place. She loved it when I was on the Opry. Mother would beam in the audience or inch close to the TV. One time I was getting ready for my eight minutes, and the audience was packed. I asked why. They told me Garth Brooks was performing that night (so technically, I can say I once opened for Garth). We were backstage and he was so nice. Someone took a picture of me with him, and I immediately had it made into an 8x10 photo for Mom to cherish. Trouble is, she insisted on using a 5x7 frame given to her by someone in her Sunday School class. Her solution—she cut Garth out! She had no idea who he was. So there on her wall was a picture of me and some guy's arm around me, unattached to the body and the hat.

A few months later, I was performing in Florida and THE Reverend Billy Graham, the most famous evangelist in America and an adviser to presidents, was there. You'd better believe I made sure to get my picture taken with Dr. Graham and sent the 8x10 to Mom. She went to Walmart and bought a brand-new 5x7 frame. Yep, there were the pictures. Side by side. Except this time, she cut me out of the picture!

Mom also tried to write a book. Why not? I had written a few. She called one night and said, "I'm going to write a book and put it on your merchandise table, and I want you to send me my money each week." She titled it *Treasures from the Junk Drawer*, and it was the shortest autobiography ever written. At the time, David was an English professor, and he spent most of his days grading college essays and spent his nights editing Mom's book. I don't think he would have given her a good grade. One night while David was sitting in bed with his red ink pen, he nudged me and said, "Honey, you have got to read this." I think my mom was trying to say that sometimes life will drain the happiness right out of you. Maybe she was saying the joy gets sucked out of you. But what she wrote was "those happy sucking days."

We circulated that paragraph around to the whole family, then we waited until the right time to bust her chops about her phrase. The following Thanksgiving, after we went around the room and said what we were thankful for, and after our prayer of gratitude, we all raised our glasses and shouted, "Happy Suckings!" Mother just sat there and said, "Well, I tell you the truth. All of ya'll suck!" She knew that would shock us all to death, and it did! And we all cracked up.

I am so proud of my mom for surviving and building a good life for herself. She started wearing slacks when she was forty-five. The hussy! At age sixty-two, she got her ears pierced. Trollop! At around sixty-five, she was diagnosed with cancer. It was grueling. There were close calls, but she beat it back while still working as a nurse. Almost twenty years later, pain in her gut led her to get an ultrasound in which we happily discovered that it was not the return of cancer but a large benign tumor due to diverticulitis that required a colostomy bag until her bowels could heal. (And yes, I told her often, "I knew you were 'full of it'! Now I have the pictures to prove it!") But at eighty-four years old, she grossed us all out by complaining it interfered with her love life.

During the reversal surgery, the surgeon nicked her bowel, and she in turn got sepsis. My brother and I barely left her side in the seven weeks before she died. I loved my mother more than air. And I spent all my last days with her telling her so. I wanted her to know how much I admired her and her resilience after all she had been through.

She rarely acknowledged that she had lived a hard life. Mainly because I don't think she ever thought that she did. A painful divorce from a man repeatedly unfaithful to her, losing her identity as a pastor's wife, losing not one but two beautiful daughters. My mother would just pat my hand and tell me, "Oh honey, what you're going through with your girl is so much worse."

I sat by her side most often during the night. She was restless in the last days. Her mumbles and moans rarely made sense. One night I said, "What's wrong Mom? You can't get comfortable?" She said with great clarity, sounding almost disappointed, "I thought I was gone. I thought I was getting to go." A day later, Mother was gone.

There is no better story to illustrate why I admire my mother so much than the day she and I took her grandkids to the cemetery. She was just barely seventy years old and surviving cancer. She loved to put flowers on the girls' graves during the holidays. In Tennessee, Memorial Day is often referred to as Decoration Day. It's almost like a contest to see who can decorate a grave the best. On this Memorial Day, it probably wasn't the safest thing for Mother to do. She was deep into heavy rounds of chemotherapy after having a mastectomy. But she insisted on going and wanted to take her grandkids along. So off we went to the cemetery with a load of flowers. I know what you're thinking—a cemetery is not necessarily the place you want to take someone who is fighting to stay alive, but that is where she insisted on going.

She dolled up in her brand-new Eva Gabor wig. She said she didn't want the grandkids to be worried about her if they saw her bald head. (I think she just wanted to show off how cute she was in her new blue jeans and fancy wig!)

Mom, her four grandchildren, and I picked up a bucket of fried chicken and drove to Forest Hills Cemetery. (I know, it's a little weird. But people picnic with the dead on Decoration Day, a.k.a. Memorial Day.) The kids were much younger then, and spending the day out of school at a cemetery with a bucket of chicken probably sounded like something out of a Harry Potter story to them.

Just as Mom bent down to place flowers on a grave, a gust of wind blew the wig off her head. At first, we all just froze. Mom's grandsons simply started rolling in the grass. My daughter ran to Mother's side to comfort her in case she was embarrassed. Me, being the most tender and sensitive of all her children said, "Mom! It's fine! You look like Yoda!" Mother hunched over, hiding her ears with her hands as the boys started chasing down her wig. It rolled like a tumbleweed across the cemetery. Suddenly, Mom decided to join the boys.

There she was, in her seventies, with cancer, chasing a wig over tombstone after tombstone until she finally got it back. Her oldest grandson, Josh, caught the wig, I began to pull the grass out of it, and we stood in our little circle trying to protect mother from onlookers until we could get it back on her head. Her shoulders were heaving up and down. I was worried about an asthma attack or the stress on her heart. I thought maybe she was hiding her face because she was crying. "Mom, are you okay? It's fine, Mother. I don't think anyone saw anything."

Mom raised her head. She wasn't crying at all. She was laughing. Laughing so hard that she could barely catch her breath.

She then squared her shoulders, lifted her head, and declared, "Well, I guess as long as I can chase my hair, I'm still alive."

What is that? How did she always do that? It wasn't deflection to mask pain. It had been too many years for that to work anymore. What is that "thing" that keeps your head above water? If I could bottle it and give it to you, I would in a heartbeat.

Early one morning after Mother died, I rolled over in a hotel room. The closed door was a complete mirror, and I glanced at my matted hair and sagging, tired eyes and snapped a picture of myself. I sent it to my brother, typing, "She lives!"

The older I get, the more I become the spitting image of my mom, from my fat knees to my bulging hips. I have her chins (yes, plural), her curly thinning hair, and her stubby fingers. I *am* my mother's daughter. And, I say proudly, I have that thing that always bounces back—that white-knuckle faith that you almost dare someone to take from you, that thing that makes you know that life could always be worse, and there is always someone worse off than you are. It is the unapologetic courage to hope.

Because life is funny . . . until it's not. And then it is again.

# ACKNOWLEDGMENTS

When you write a book about your whole life, how do you recall the name of every person who helped you survive your life? It's almost impossible. First of all, this book is for YOU the reader, the people who bought tickets, T-shirts, videos, and DVDs. You have given me a purpose. We have pursued laughter and God together. The laughter will fade, but GOD will bind us together until His return.

There are just a few individuals I must mention:

Jerry and Ann Huff—You have been my cousins, parents, guardians, and friends. I love you.

Johnny and Shirley Jones, my Ashland City parents, and Teresa—You are my family.

Julie Lockert Hibbs—You are my big sister by choice.

Glynda Maxey—You have been my bestie, my assistant, my stylist, and I am grateful for ALL of it.

There are men who showed me true leadership and integrity. You have changed my life, helped me grow spiritually, and taught me there really are good guys in the world:

Pastor Shiloh Hackett

Pastor Allen Jackson

Governor Mike Huckabee

James Robison

Jeff Biederman

And then, there are the countless people who care about what I do: producers, radio personalities, and record company folks. But the promoter who has done more for me than anyone can imagine is Dan Fife. Also, thank you to every road manager, venue, and bus driver.

My Girlfriends—You are my tribe and my muse. Thank you for your unconditional love. Julie, Judith, Patrice, Necie, Kim, Meribeth, Mary, Glynda, Melanie—You are my sisters by choice.

Jon Macks and Alice Crider—You are the folks who helped me get this story out of my mouth and onto the page.

The team that keeps me pulled together: Dawn Nepp, Tommy McBride, Tracey Robinson. Much love to my "adopted" kiddos: Fabiano, Bone, and Drew. Thank you to: Seattle and Nessa for showing me that I would have been a good grandma!

My manager, Andrew Tenenbaum—No one else has survived the tornado that is ME! Not only did YOU give me validation to believe I am funny, you protected me, guided me, and built a career out of this clean country comic that has exceeded all my expectations. Now, lose my number—I'm tired!!!

And last but never least: My son, David Zachary Pierce—We survived life together. You challenged me. You built me up. You exasperated me. But you never stopped loving me. I have never been prouder of anything in my life than simply being your mother.

## PERMISSIONS

All Scripture quotations, unless otherwise indicated, are taken from the Holy Bible, New International Version®, NIV®. Copyright © 1973, 1978, 1984, 2011 by Biblica, Inc.® Used by permission of Zondervan. All rights reserved worldwide. www.zondervan.com. The "NIV" and "New International Version" are trademarks registered in the United States Patent and Trademark Office by Biblica, Inc.®

Scriptures marked KJV are taken from the King James Version, public domain.

"Whatever It Takes" (Wolfe Lanny Music Company / Capitol CMG)Copyright © 1975 Lanny Wolfe Music (ASCAP) (adm. at CapitolCMGPublishing.com). All rights reserved. Used by permission.

"Chasing Rebels" (Curb Records Inc.) Chasing Rebels written by Tony Wood, Michael Farren and Ben Fuller. Courtesy of Curb Congregation Songs I Tony Wood Songs (adm. by Curb Congregation Songs), I Wolf Brigade Music (adm. by Curb Congregation Songs)/ Essential Music Publishing.

"Chasing Rebels" (Essential Music Publishing) © 2022 Ben Fuller Music (BMI) / Be Essential Songs (BMI) (adm. at EssentialMusicPublishing.com). All rights reserved. Used by permission.

"The Saving Kind" (Capitol CMG) Copyright © 2001 Universal Music—Brentwood Benson Publ. (ASCAP) (adm. at CapitolCMGPublishing.com). All rights reserved. Used by permission.

"Even If" (Ariose Music Group Inc. / Capitol CMG) Copyright © 2017 Ariose Music (ASCAP) Universal Music—Brentwood Benson Publ. (ASCAP) (adm. at CapitolCMGPublishing.com). All rights reserved. Used by permission.

"Even If" (Spirit Music Group) Words and Music by Bart Millard, David Garcia, Ben Glover, Tim Timmons, and Crystal Lewis © 2017 Spirit Two Nashville (ASCAP), Universal Music – Brentwood Benson Publishing (ASCAP), Ariose Music (ASCAP), Tunes of MercyMe (SESAC), All Essential Music (ASCAP), LetsBeBeautiful (ASCAP), and Crystallized (ASCAP). Universal Music—Brentwood Benson Publ. and Ariose Music (adm. at capitolcmgpublishing.com), Tunes of MercyMe, All Essential Music, and LetsBeBeautiful (adm. at essentialmusicpublishing.com), Crystallized (adm. by Music Services). All Rights Reserved. Used by Permission. Reprinted by Permission of Hal Leonard LLC

"Even If" (Provident Music Group / Essential Music Publishing) © 2017 Tunes of MercyMe (SESAC) / All Essential Music (ASCAP) / Letsbebeautiful (ASCAP) (adm. at EssentialMusicPublishing.com). All rights reserved. Used by permission.

Unless otherwise indicated, all photos are used with permission by the author.